DOCUMENTATION STANDARDS

GRA

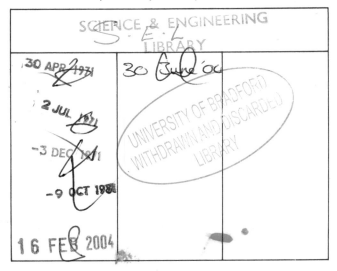

DOCUMENTATION STANDARDS

MAX GRAY
and
KEITH LONDON

BUSINESS BOOKS LIMITED
London

PRINTED IN THE UNITED STATES OF AMERICA

PREFACE

The purpose of this book is to provide to data processing managers, supervisors, and analysts a practical guide for the design and implementation of a standard system of documentation for data processing.

The rate at which computerized information handling systems are being installed is overwhelming. Computers are now the rule rather than the exception in business organizations. As with any popular modern technology, a new thriving industry has been created, with its own terminology, its own job titles—and its own mystique. From the small beginnings of a computerized unit record installation, we have progressed to installations abounding in a multiplicity of job titles such as analyst—job/procedures/methods, systems—analyst/designer/engineer, programmer—coder/utility/maintenance/applications, and so on, with a proportionate abundance of controllers, supervisors, and managers.

With the greater degree of job specialization, the increase in complexity of hardware, the proliferation of programming languages, and the wider range of applications, the industry is facing a crucial communication problem: A greater volume of information of higher complexity passes among growing numbers of people of dissimilar backgrounds. In such a working environment, some attempt must be made to rationalize the information flow in the development of a data processing system. A state of anarchy (or near anarchy) would exist if each individual had to decide

- if he would record anything at all
- what information he would record at any one time in a development project

v

- what information he would supply to the next person in the development process

- the content, form, and level of detail of the information recorded.

Obviously, there must be some agreed level of communication; essentially this must be a definition of who prepares what document, when and how.

The primary objectives of this book are

- to define the purposes and types of documentation, and to assign responsibilities for preparatory review and approval of documentation

- to describe the role and content of documentation within systems development

- to show the importance of documentation in project control

- to emphasize the importance of documentation standards and to outline methods of developing these standards

- to outline a model documentation system.

Acknowledgements

This book has drawn on the experience of developing documentation standards for many companies. We would like to acknowledge material drawn from the manual of Data Processing Standard of the Standard Telephones and Cables Ltd; the material used in pages 71 et seq and in Appendices B and C was based on this publication.

CONTENTS

CHAPTER 1

Background to Data Processing Documentation

This chapter presents a general background to the topic of data processing documentation by providing basic definitions and a discussion on the purposes and types of documentation that are commonly recognized. Based on the background framework presented in this chapter, a detailed presentation of various document types will be given. The chapter concludes with a general summary and a description of the layout of the book.

DEFINITIONS

For the purposes of this book, data processing documentation can be defined as an organized series of descriptive documents relating to all aspects of system development and operation. A document is further defined as a written record of the completion of a phase of work. Within the broad definition of documentation as given above, a further breakdown of types of documentation may be made. Basically documentation may be categorized into *development documentation* and *control documentation*. Development documentation is descriptive of a system itself, i.e., a system's operating performance characteristics, tools and materials. Development documentation is therefore the means of communicating information *about* the system.

Control documentation on the other hand is concerned with communicating information about resources used to develop the system; it is therefore primarily concerned with project development organization, with personnel, time, materials and money.

PURPOSES OF DOCUMENTATION

The purposes of documentation may be categorized into

- Inter task/phase communication
- Quality control
- Historical reference
- Instructional

Inter Task/Phase Communication

It has long been recognized that poor or inadequate communication between personnel is a major problem area. For example, a user (i.e., the service or operating department) advocating a new system or change to a system has an idea which he must communicate to a systems analyst. The systems analyst must in turn communicate the program requirements to the programmer, who must specify how the computer operators must run the program, and so on. Invariably, without adequate documentation, as in the old "telephone game," the initial idea from the user becomes distorted, the final product bearing little relation to the original intention. Planned standard documentation intends to eliminate this element of distortion by permitting the orderly communication of ideas from one project phase to another.

At a lower level, standard documentation facilitates good communication between project personnel engaged in the same phase. The assignment of personnel can be a great problem area. First there is the now classic data processing employee turnover syndrome. With current predictions of staff shortages (e.g., ———— unfilled positions for programmers, rising to _____ in ten years), there is a high turnover of technical personnel. Various estimates give the average length of stay for programmers as being in the order of 14–16 months. In this environment, planned standard documentation would reduce the impact of staff turnover.

Similarly, flexibility of personnel assignment whereby staff may be reassigned to another project before completion (to make use of special skills and requirements) can only be achieved if there is the minimum of disruption in task turnover.

Quality Control and Project Control

As in the manufacture or creation of any other product, the product of data processing development—the system—must be reviewed not only at implementation but also throughout its development. The only viable method of quality control review in development is to study and assess the product through its documentation as it proceeds from concept to general design and ultimately into operational form.

A good system of documentation not only specifies how information is to be recorded, but also when it is to be recorded. If the system of documentation specifies that documents are to be completed concurrently with tasks, the completion of a task is signified by the availability of the finalized documents. A review of completed documentation thus provides a means for assessing progress and points out inconsistencies between scheduled dates and actual dates. It will also provide for a current assessment of the amount of development work in progress.

A further aspect of standard documentation in this field is in the area of project control. Often data processing management is unable or finds it not feasible to provide regular supervision for the development of a particular system. Documentation describing a system at each step becomes almost indispensable, because it establishes design and performance criteria to be met during subsequent phases of project work. Using standard documentation, the programming or systems analysis supervisory function can constantly review work to ensure that it meets all the requirements specified. Management can then limit its review to certain specific delineated project control points. Project control thus becomes a built-in function of documentation and provides a medium for the verification of the satisfactory completion of work performed.

This frees management from the "policing"-type role and also makes increased organizational control and discipline an inherent characteristic of the system development process.

Historical Reference

Documentation functions as a source for historical reference and the provision of a permanent record of work performed. Thus reference can be made for

- modifications and improvements to an existing system
- drawing on past experience in the development of jobs similar to work that has been done before

A system or program is a dynamic entity—as businesses grow and strive to improve their operations, systems must be enhanced. Because of the various combinations and permutations of conditions in a program, one cannot always assume that a program has been adequately tested and is totally free from error. Therefore, it is evident that changes may be required after a system or program is in operation.

One of the most time-consuming activities for a programmer can be trying to understand a program that he coded sometime in the past or that another programmer coded. Nothing can be more frustrating to a programmer than to study the documentation to a program, undertake to make changes on the basis of the information given in the documentation, and then to find that some prior changes have not been documented, thus invalidating the new changes. Adequate documentation, properly maintained, is a necessity for efficient system and program updates. Similarly, adequate documentation of programs previously developed is a necessity for the conversion of a system to new machines. Often, the logical flow of a system is independent of machine type. Common logical functions can be found on different machines or machine configurations; the differences lie in the manner in which the coded instructions cause machines to perform these functions. Therefore, the bulk of the work in a machine conversion is often in the recoding of the programs with a minimum of new systems analysis and of new program logic design.

The historical record provided by adequate documentation can serve as a valuable pool of experience in the development of future systems. Examination of the documentation of systems developed previously can prove valuable in the development of similar systems or systems which are expansions of existing processing. The main areas in which such a review could prove useful are system methodology, project control and progress.

A common characteristic of initiating a systems development job is that a seemingly urgent need for a system turns it into a "rush job." The general result is that the actual design work for a job is begun too quickly, without adequate analysis and review of previous development work. A review of available information may reveal that previously developed data files can be used in the proposed system; the techniques and methodology used in one system may be suitable for application to a new system, thereby obviating the development of new techniques. The time criteria for early delivery takes precedence over the development of special, dedicated techniques. In the long run, therefore, the development of systems without adequate planning and review can be more costly and time consuming than if more time and resources were spent on the initial planning phase.

Obviously, where a proposed system interfaces with a previously developed system, it is vital to review the interaction between the two systems. This can only be satisfactorily achieved if the previously designed system is adequately documented.

In the area of project control and review, reference to progress records of similar completed projects can be useful for evaluating schedules and deadlines for a new project. Special problem areas discovered in previous development projects will enable special provision of time and resources to be made in anticipating similar situations on a new project.

During actual project work, comparisons can be made between the developmental stages of the present project and the comparable phases of previous projects as a form of assessing achievement and improvement. If the historical control documentation is adequate and has been sensibly reviewed, the setting and meeting of schedules and dates of past projects should certainly be improved on in subsequent projects. This improvement should be especially significant if methodology and information used in existing systems is applied to new projects. Thus, the degree of efficient development of the new system over the previous system will be measured by the degree of improvement.

Instructional Reference

The last of the purposes of documentation is the use of documentation as an instructional device. We have seen that adequate documentation is essential if good communication is to be maintained between data processing personnel. It can also serve a general instruction function for communication between the data processing specialists and the non-specialists, principally the users. In the modern environment of data processing, there is certainly no case for perpetuating the "closed circle" mystique of data processing. It is vital that users have a clear understanding of their system for only by doing so is it possible to establish good user relations and to enable the user to apply a system intelligently. This is best achieved by evaluating a minimum level of adequate documentation needed to inform the user about the application of his system.

Within the scope of the above discussion it is difficult to conceive of a data processing environment which does not recognize that the four purposes of documentation are axiomatic to its existence. Or that the six fundamental categories (following) are basic to the operation of any data processing department. Yet such organizations do exist. Perhaps they exist in their present form because of the "rush-job" concept—do now, document later, but later never comes. Alternatively, perhaps such organizations exist because of the false economics of achieving short term objectives. Experienced project personnel are constantly assigned to projects, the data processing manager is permanently tied down as arbitrator between users or with budgetary problems and thus no one can be spared for the task of reviewing documentation.

As observed in this chapter, documentation is the means to communicate; but how can any organization, data processing or otherwise, exist without a common agreed level of communication. Thus, adequate documentation is probably the primary contributing factor towards maximizing efficiency in a data processing installation. Similarly, the converse of poor uncoordinated documentation limiting efficiency also holds true.

TYPES OF DOCUMENTATION

Thus far, we have established some basic definitions and examined the primary purposes and objectives of establishing a planned system of adequate documentation. It is now possible to define the elementary types of documentation in relation to the various data processing tasks. Data processing documentation as has been shown serves many distinct functions; in addition, it can be categorized into six distinct applicational areas

- Analytical
- System
- Program
- Operations
- User aids
- Management aids

A general summary illustrating the sequence of document preparation related to development workflow is given in Figure 2.1. Each of the types of documentation listed above are defined below. The relationship between these documents and to the working environment is discussed in Chapter 2.

Analytical

Analytical documentation can be defined as that recording and reporting which must precede any systems design or programming work. Principally, it consists of a written and approved statement of the nature and objectives of the project. It may include

- a user request stating the problem,
- an evaluation of the feasibility of the requested system,
- an estimate of development time and resources required, and
- a statement of the objectives and parameters of the proposed system.

System

System documentation encompasses all information needed to define the proposed data processing system to a level that it can be programmed, tested and implemented. The major document is a system specification which acts as the permanent record of the structure, functions, flow and control of the system. It is the basic medium of communication of information about the proposed system between the systems design, programming and user functions.

Program

Program documentation comprises the records of the detailed logic and coding of the constituent programs of a system. It is prepared by the programmer and aids

- Trouble-shooting
- Program maintenance
- Machine conversion
- Programmer change-over

Program documentation covers both specific application programs and general purpose or in-house developed software. Documentation for the latter may require a special level of detail, but in principle, all program types would be covered by the same general rules of documentation.

Operations

Operations documentation specifies those procedures required for the running of the system by data processing operations personnel. It gives the general sequence of events for performing the job and defines precise procedures for

- Data control and security
- Data preparation
- Program running
- Output dispersal
- Ancillary operations

User Aids

User aids comprise all descriptive and instructive material necessary for the user to participate in the running of the operational system. They include principally instructions and schedules for the collection and preparation of data prior to submission to data processing operations, and explanatory notes on the content, review and distribution of material.

Management Aids

Management aids are that type of documentation which provides management with non-technical instructive information. They enable management to evaluate the applicability of a system to a requirement and provide sufficient information to enable management to participate in the operational systems.

SUMMARY

1. Documentation is defined as the collection of reports relating to a complete system.

2. Two categories of documentation are recognized: development documentation, which records information *about a system,* and control documentation, which records information *about a system development project.* In this book, we are primarily concerned with development documentation.

3. Documentation has four main purposes:

- Inter task/phase communication
- Quality control
- Historical reference
- Instructional reference

4. The six basic classifications of documentation are

- Analytical
- System
- Program
- Operations
- User aids
- Management aids

ORGANIZATION OF THE BOOK

The next chapter in Part I of the book relates the classification of types of documents to the structure and general environment of the development organization. Part II presents a detailed analysis of the six types of development documentation as defined above, and relates them to a model documentation system. Part III describes the application of documentation in terms of establishing project control points, a documentation library and methods of documentation maintenance.

CHAPTER 2

Documentation in a Working Environment

FACTORS DETERMINING DOCUMENTATION USAGE

Documentation is concerned with communication. The paths of communication in a data processing department depend upon many factors, namely

- management commitment,
- the characteristics of the projects (number, duration and complexity),
- the organization structure, and
- the technical environment.

Since all the above factors vary from data processing department to data processing department, it is obvious that there is no ideal universal set of documentation standards. The type and level of complexity of documentation for one location may be totally invalid in another environment. Each data processing department must therefore implement a documentation system which suits its own environment. Since it is often possible to adopt documentation from various sources, the impact of the above factors on documentation is discussed below.

Management Commitment

This is the degree to which management realizes the necessity for good documentation. It includes the time and resources that management is prepared to expend on developing and enforcing documentation standards. In general, therefore, the quality and completeness of documentation is directly affected by the extent to which management is committed to documentation.

Before embarking on a documentation standards program, it may well be necessary to first convince management of the importance of documentation. In some industries, particularly the service industries, projects are undertaken on a "random" basis, subject only to client standards and approval. In these circumstances, management may find it difficult to understand why rigid standards of documentation are necessary. Other types of businesses may be more accustomed to good record keeping. In such cases, proper documentation standards in data processing would be more readily accepted.

The management commitment will of course influence the attitude of project personnel. Often, in the course of implementing a system, data processing management itself can often influence user management against documentation standards. The classic example of this is the two-choice approach: "We can implement the system in six months with documentation or four months without." The act of implementing rigid documentation requirements can raise cries of longer project times, as if adequate documentation is an expensive luxury. Management must thus be presented with the simple argument, "Can we afford *not* to document effectively?"

Project Characteristics

The amount and complexity of documentation is a function of the characteristics of the projects handled. The most influential characteristics are length of project development time and the size of project teams. In Chapter 1, one of the purposes of development documentation was that it could be used as a guide in assessing project progress. For projects of long duration, documentation must be created at all crucial stages of development. Thus, the greater the required level of documentation, the better the control over a lengthy project. Similarly, the larger the project team, the greater the need for an adequate level of documentation to facilitate ease of communication.

Projects of long duration or requiring large numbers of personnel therefore require more documentation than a project of shorter duration in order to maintain adequate control and good communication.

The importance, frequency of use and life expectancy of a system are also influential factors in determining documentation requirements. A system which will only be used once or for a very limited period would not normally require the same level of documentation as a system intended for much longer use. In how many cases, however, does the "temporary" or "one-time" system become "permanent" or "many-time?" Will the "temporary" or "one-time" system form the basis for a more permanent solution? For example, if a program is developed on the assumption that its life would be limited, say by the very nature of the application, extensive documentation would be unnecessary. Moreover, if the short life was based on organizational functions, such as equipment changes, then other aspects of the program documentation would need to be stressed. Emphasis would be placed on development documentation showing program logic and methodology so that the program for the new equipment could be based on the techniques and logic in the temporary program.

As discussed in Chapter 1, computer systems are dynamic. Changes become necessary as users revise their requirements, new software or hardware techniques become available, and errors in the original system are discovered. These changes often begin to originate early in the development phase and continue throughout the life of the system. The area most susceptible to such changes is programming.

It is a reasonably safe assumption that changes to long life programs are assured. These changes, whether they be for error correction or program enhancement, can only be properly implemented if there is adequate and well-maintained program documentation.

Not only is the number of data processing personnel on a project important; the number of users is also an influencing factor. If many people are to have access to a system, it would be of great importance to have very complete documentation. A system catering to few users would probably require a lesser degree of documentation detail.

Corporate Environment and Structure

At its simplest level, one of the most active influences on the level and type of documentation is the general working environment of the company and its organizational structure. A military installation with the general requirement for exact and complete documentation in minute detail would automatically require the same approach to data processing documentation. The requirements for documentation would also reflect the rigid complex organization of command. On the same principle, a small general service industry with a loose system of documentation and/or reporting structure would have, without strong management, a loose system of data processing documentation.

Thus, in a data processing organization with precisely defined job functions and a large number of personnel will require a greater level of documentation than a small, rather loosely organized unit.

Large companies with a number of decentralized data processing organizations, each with its own development capability, generally have an interchange of ideas among the organizations. Similar types of projects may be developed at various locations. Adequate documentation is invaluable if there is not to be a duplication of effort in developing like applications independently.

Technical Environment

The technical environment is taken to be those factors which influence the manner in which project personnel work. Such factors are:

- software and hardware available,
- level of technical competence, and
- communication problems due to geographical distances.

To a large extent, hardware is not a major influence on the type of level of documentation. Obviously, an installation using data transmission links or with a large ancillary support to the computer(s) will require more documentation than an installation with only one small computer configuration. The difference is thus in terms of volume rather than document types.

Similarly, the software environments do have some influence on documentation. Because of their similarity to the English language, high-level languages require less detailed technical program documentation than low-level languages. Further, the form of the system documentation may be dependent on language used. For example, files may be specified at system design time in terms of the data defining method of a specific language.

An installation using manufacturer-supplied application packages should be provided with at least outline documentation, which will include the specification of system parameters. Users will generally augment the manufacturer supplied subroutines by specialized operational subroutines for their particular needs. These subroutines for general use must be described in detail if they are to be available to all programmers in an installation and possibly other installations.

DOCUMENTATION PREPARATION

It is necessary to establish a very generalized organizational structure and project development scheme on which the subsequent documentation types may be based.

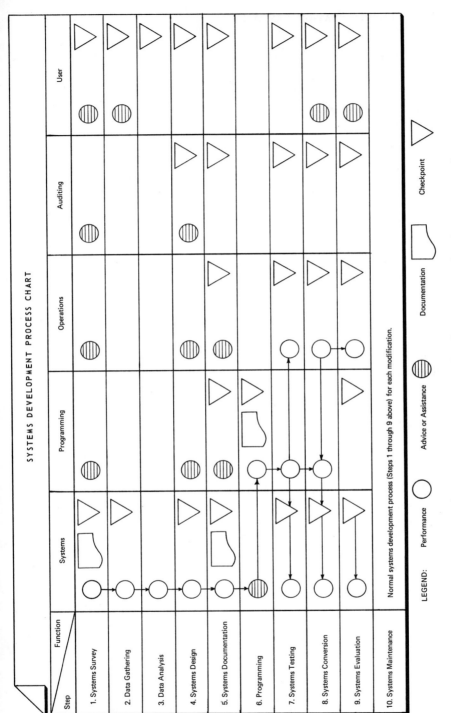

Figure 2-1 Sequence of document preparation in a systems development project

The first phase in a development project can be considered as Project Initiation comparing such tasks:

- Project selection
- Project authorization
- Planning
- Personnel assignment
- Estimating
- Scheduling
- Budgeting

This phase may be said to produce all or most of the analytical documentation. The next phase is project fulfillment, covering systems design work and programming.

The systems design tasks will produce systems documentation, some data processing operations documentation, and user and management aids. The programming work results in the preparation of programming documentation and some operations documentation (i.e., computer operating instructions). The final phase, Project Conclusion, includes conversion and a post-implementation audit; in effect, no development documentation is produced, but the validity of the current documentation is checked. The overall sequence of documentation preparation in terms of a systems development project is shown in Figure 2.1.

SUMMARY

1. There are no universal documentation standards which are directly applicable to all installations.

2. Documentation must thus be developed for individual installations. This can be done adopting general documentation systems, such as the one presented in this book, to local conditions.

3. The development of a documentation system for a particular data processing organization must take account of the major influencing factors which are

- management commitment,
- project characteristics,
- corporate environment and organization structure, and
- technical environment.

CHAPTER 3

Analytical Documentation

At the beginning of a development project, prior to the commencement of actual development work, a written and approved statement defining the proposed project should be prepared. Analytical documentation serves this function by stating the nature, objectives, and evaluation of the requested work.

The suggested analytical documentation presented in this chapter is comprised of these documents:

- a User Request,
- a Systems Proposal,
- an Analytical Report, and
- a Design Requirement Statement,

although, as explained below, the Analytical Report, Systems Proposal, and Design Requirements Statement present three different approaches. Before considering each of these documents in detail, it is first necessary to define the general relationship between them.

The User Request defines the problem area in outline and presents a formal notification that data processing assistance is required. The Systems Proposal is a preliminary description of the problem, the problem environment and a proposed approach to a problem solution. It thus includes a feasibility analysis. The Analytical Report is a detailed description of the project; i.e., responsibility allocation, resource requirements and project schedules. The Design Requirements Statement is a detailed description of the objectives and parameters of the proposed system for the subsequent system development work.

To summarize the purposes of the four documents:

1. User Request
   - initial problem definition and request for data processing assistance

2. Systems Proposal
   - further problem definition and solution feasibility analysis

3. Analytical Report
   - definition of project work required to implement selected solution.

4. Design Requirements Statement
   - detailed specification of the selected solution for subsequent development work (i.e., systems design *et al.*).

Thus the User Request and Systems Proposal are used to establish a project and as such form an agreed method for communication between user and data processing personnel. The Analytical Report and Design Requirements Statement perform a similar function, but by defining what is to be done and how it is to be done, they additionally form an agreed method for communication between the system analysis and project planning functions, and between the system design and subsequent functions.

In practice, the User Request and at least an outline Analytical Report are almost always required. Generally, the Systems Proposal and Design Requirements Statement are only produced for major development projects or for extensive system modifications.

The degree of detail presented in these documents will depend on the complexity of the problem and the amount of new development work required. For example, most one-time reports produced from existing data sources in previously implemented systems may require the production of a full User Request and limited Analytical Report only. On the other hand, the design and creation of a complete new system or major new file in an existing system may require the production of all four reports in detail.

The remainder of this chapter describes the purpose, contents and use of the four analytical documents. Note however that the types of documents prepared and the actual sequence of preparations depends upon the organization structure and assignment of responsibilities in a particular installation. To show the use of the documents in relation to a working environment, the following is a brief description of the "traditional" process flow.

1. Informal discussion between user management and data processing management.

2. Submission of User Request by the user, probably prepared with systems analysis assistance to ensure completeness.

3. Initial review of User Request and assignment of analyst effort to prepare Systems Proposal, *if required*. Note that the Systems Proposal may be a major task, requiring a thorough investigation of a major applicational area. The systems proposal is thus *problem* oriented and will form the basis for the subsequent project-oriented Analytical Report.

4. Submission of Systems Proposal and evaluation of project feasibility.

5. Analytical Report prepared by systems analysis function covering the area specified in the User Request or, if prepared, Systems Proposal. Note that the Analytical Report may be prepared directly after the discussion of the User Request, (3) above. This would take place if the problem area is essentially local, non-complex and previously well defined. In effect, therefore, a brief Systems Proposal would be incorporated in the Analytical Report.

6. If the project is to be undertaken, approve the outline specification in the Systems Proposal and Analytical Report and agree outline schedules and costs.

7. Prepare, *if necessary,* a Design Requirements Statement for the subsequent development work. Note that the description of a system approach given in the Systems Proposal may form a basis for the subsequent design work.

8. Commence detailed project planning, e.g., schedules, resource allocation, budget controls forming the Project Plan.

USER REQUEST

The first formal approach to initiate a project is made by the submission of a User Request. This is prepared by the user, although for complex problems, assistance may be given by the systems analysis function to ensure completeness. A list of standard items that should appear in the report is given below. To ensure that all the required information is provided, consideration should be given to devising a standard form to guide non-technical users. The provision of standard forms however is usually only necessary when significant volumes of requests are anticipated.

The User Request may contain the following information.

Identification and Authority—This is a clear identification of the proponent and states the authority for the request.

Problem Definition—The Problem Definition contains a succinct statement of the problem. This generally includes
Objectives—a statement of the objectives of the work requested: what it will do, whom it will serve, how it is related to the current method (e.g., the report or process to be replaced or supported)
Data Sources—the anticipated source of data
Data Output—brief description of the output desired
Timing—the date by which the request is to be satisfied, together with other significant dates

References—The content of this section will depend on local conditions; it may contain, for example, the persons to be contacted for further information or a list of attached or available studies or backup material of known or potential value to the systems analyst.

The degree of detail given in the problem definition will depend on the degree of familiarity of the user with data processing in general, with his applications in particular, and the amount of assistance provided by the systems analyst. For the production of a report in an existing system, for example, the user should be able to specify

- Report title
- Frequency, date of production and effective date of content
- Title or headings desired
- Number of copies and distribution
- Sequence of items, and intermediate and final totals desired

For a new system or application, the report will probably be prepared largely by the systems analyst working in conjunction with the user since many major projects are initiated by the incentive data processing staff rather than the user.

SYSTEMS PROPOSAL

The Systems Proposal is a preliminary description of a proposed approach to the project. It is generally prepared by the systems analyst. The Systems Proposal is primarily a study of the problem environment; it is thus a review of current system philosophy and methods, and requirements for the new system.

A document of this nature must be an optional document, since it will only be produced for a major project. The review of a total applicational area, for example, may represent a major project phase, especially if the system under consideration covers many areas of a company's operations. This review phase may be called the "systems survey." Obviously, the systems survey phase as such would not be required for projects of limited scope. In this case, the outline problem definition in the User Request would be adequate as a basis for future development work.

The content of the Systems Proposal may be summarized as follows. It contains

- The design approach
- Brief analysis of the present environment
- Plan and schedule for implementation

A sample list of contents is given below. This example shows the Systems Proposal at the highest level of detail, i.e., for a major development project as described above.

This example is based on a six-part document comprising

1.0 Introduction
2.0 Management Summary
3.0 Design Alternatives
4.0 Proposed System Description
5.0 Outline Implementation Plan and Schedule
6.0 Graphics and Appendices.

Eventually, the Introduction is a purely housekeeping section while the Management Summary summarizes the detail of the remainder of the report. Section 3, Design alternatives, briefly describes all the possible approaches to "solving the problem." The Proposed System Description defines, in reasonable detail, the selected or at this stage, the recommended approach to the solution. Section 4, Implementation Plan and Schedule, describes how the recommended approach described in Section 3 may be implemented.

The Systems Proposal therefore presents a detailed system feasibility study.

Introduction

This consists of a summary of the conditions under which the systems survey was performed.

Scope of Study—the purpose, objectives, background and limitations of the study taken from the initial Users Request.

Methods—the methods used in the systems survey and preparation of the Systems Proposal.

Premises and Assumptions—the basic ground rules or actions under which the study is conducted.

Management Summary

The Management Summary contains three categories of information
   (a) Findings
   (b) Recommendations
   (c) Plan of Action

The *Findings* describes the current environment. A suggested breakdown is as follows:

Summary—a list of the strengths and weaknesses of the organization and procedures as related to the project

Organization and Functions—present organizational and functional flowchart

Present Systems—data processing systems: evaluation of their cost and effectiveness

Present Systems—non-data processing systems: are they efficient, accurate, and meeting their requirements?

Information Requirements—definition of present and future information requirements

Personnel—evaluation of the capability of staff to handle new system(s)

The *Recommendations* presents such information as

Information Requirements—system approach in terms of the criteria for purpose, e.g., short range, intermediate range, and long range plans. The recommended information requirements are compared to the original requirements (e.g., as defined in the User Request).

Advantages and Disadvantages—The advantages and disadvantages of the proposed system are listed and compared with the existing or alternative systems in terms of

- services
- equipment and facilities
- organization

Costs—a cost comparison, in the form of a table, showing the following items for at least a five-year period

- development cost of new system by kind of personnel equipment used and capital investments
- operational costs of new system
- costs of the present system (if applicable); for equipment and personnel per unit time, including anticipated system and program maintenance costs

The *Plan of Action* describes the recommended course of action based on the Recommendation given previously. It should include the following.

Management Action—the required management action in terms of

- organizational and policy decisions
- procedural changes
- approval and starting date

Systems Development—a description of the tasks, with approximate schedule, for the system development process

Equipment Consideration—any special comments on the loading of existing equipment or acquisition of new equipment

Personnel and Training—a summary of personnel resources and deployment, and the required training program

Design Alternatives

A brief description of all solutions considered should be shown, and the advantages and disadvantages of each discussed.

Proposed System Description

The System Description is a narrative definition of the proposed system. There are many ways in which such a definition may be presented. In terms of the model system presented in the book, it is suggested that an overall summary be given which shows the major functional dimensions. The major dimensions are then split down into a number of Systems Abstracts. Each abstract contains the following:

- purpose
- functions
- data requirements
- products
- users

In conclusion, a summary of critical factors affecting the development of the overall system should be presented.

Outline Implementation Plan and Schedule

This defines the tasks necessary to accomplish the recommended development work. Both data processing tasks and user participation should be listed, together with the estimated time. The anticipated elapsed time should be shown against significant project milestones. The task/time definitions should also be related to a summary resource schedule.

To establish efficient project control, a negotiated "freeze date" must be specified for system design work. Beyond this date, further changes requested by the proponent should be accepted *only with an accompanying revision in the implementation date.*

In a report of this complexity it should at least be possible to define an outline project task plan and schedule to the level of

- data gathering and analysis: by major functional areas or by major files
- system design: by major function areas
- programming: by review of system specifications
  - software selection and design
  - logic design
  - coding
  - heating
- training, conversion and implementation.

In addition a skeleton project review plan should be presented listing major project checkpoints and foreseeable management decisions.

Graphics and Appendices

These materials contain any additional information that may be required.

We may at this point summarize the usage of the Systems Proposal. If it is known from information given in the User Request that the request can be met by minor program modifications and requires little or no systems design work, the Introduction, Management Summary, Proposed System Description, and Outline Implementation Plan and Schedule will usually be sufficient, the others being present in a limited form. However, care should be taken in assigning a request as a "routine local" amendment without prior investigation to establish the impact of the change (possibly unknown to the user) on the system as a whole.

The basic guiding factor in the preparation of the Systems Proposal is that it need only be as long as it needs to be to meet its purpose. That is, to present a complete and objective statement of problems and requirements upon which decisions can be based. It may be only one or two pages long or it may be a hundred. In some cases, major sections may be omitted (as in the example given above) or the sections may be further broken down into chapters and subsections. Further, as we shall see, the Analytical Report and Design Requirements Statement form alternatives to the Systems Proposal as a whole.

ANALYTICAL REPORT

The Analytical Report is primarily an alternative to a full Systems Proposal; it may be used however to supplement or replace part of a Systems Proposal. It defines the tasks, responsibilities, implementing instructions and priorities for subsequent development work. It also includes schedules of resources (personnel and equipment) developed to provide the user with the requested support. As such, the Analytical Report in conjunction with the User Request may form all the necessary analytical documentation. Alternatively, local standards may require that an Analytical Report be produced to replace or supplement the Outline Implementation Plan and Schedule in the Systems Proposal.

A sample table of contents is shown in Figure 3.1. Note that it also contains (in Section 7—Background) some information on the evaluation of the system, subsystem or modification. Where no extensive systems survey or feasibility analysis is made, i.e., no Systems Proposal is prepared, the section should contain sufficient information on project evaluation.

The degree of detail presented in the Analytical Report will depend on the characteristics of each project.

DESIGN REQUIREMENTS STATEMENT

The Design Requirements Statement states the objectives and parameters for the project; that is, for the system, subsystem, modification, file, report or file abstract, or additional computations. It serves two purposes, namely:

- to enable the user to agree to and approve the proposed changes
- to provide a positive specification for the subsequent development work.

The Design Requirements statement is prepared

- when no Systems Proposal is prepared, *and*
- the User Request and Analytical Report do not provide enough scope to describe the requirements in systems terms, *or*
- when it is required to supplement or replace Section 4, Proposed Systems Description, in the Systems Proposal

A sample table of contents for the Design Requirements Statement is shown in Figure 3.2. The degree of detail shown in the Design Requirements Statement will depend on the characteristics of the project.

ANALYTICAL REPORT

Table of Contents

1.0 General Information

    1.1 Cover Page
    1.2 Table of Contents
    1.3 Glossary of Terms
    1.4 Glossary of Symbols
    1.5 Purpose

2.0 Administrative

    2.1 Project Team Structure
    2.2 Personnel Assignments
    2.3 D.P. Dept. Responsibilities
    2.4 Contractor Responsibilities

3.0 Principal Tasks

    3.1 Subject Matter Analysis
    3.2 DP Systems Analysis
    3.3 Data Management Analysis
    3.4 Programming
    3.5 Training
    3.6 Documenting

4.0 Staff Coordinating Instructions

    4.1 Customer Liaison
    4.2 Administrative Coordination
    4.3 D.P. Dept. Project
        Personnel coordination
    4.4 Contractor Project
        Personnel Coordination

Figure 3-1   Sample Table of Contents—Analytical Report

5.0 Priority

    5.1 Authority
    5.2 Definition
    5.3 Impact on Project
    5.4 Impact on Resources
    5.5 Recommendations

6.0 Schedules

    6.1 Development Tasks
    6.2 Administrative Reporting
    6.3 Documentation
    6.4 Training

7.0 Background

    7.1 Project/Task Library Search
    7.2 Technical Library Search
    7.3 Study and Development
        Recommendations
    7.4 Experience Requirements

Figure 3.1 (continued)

DESIGN REQUIREMENTS STATEMENT

Table of Contents

1.0   General Information

    1.1 Cover Page
    1.2 Table of Contents
    1.3 Revision Page
    1.4 References (administrative,
        correspondence, etc.)

2.0   Objectives

3.0   System Criteria

    3.1 Problem Approach
    3.2 Method of Problem Solution
    3.3 System Capabilities
    3.4 Assumptions
    3.5 Limitations and Restrictions

4.0   Data

    4.1 Definitions
    4.2 Input Sources
    4.3 Output Distributions

5.0   Glossaries

    5.1 Terms
    5.2 Symbols

6.0   Bibliography

Figure 3-2   Sample Table of Contents—Design Requirements Statement

SUMMARY

1. Analytical documentation is that documentation resulting from the initial phase of a project which establishes the project prior to subsequent development work.

2. Four documents have been described

- User Request
- Systems Proposal
- Analytical Report
- Design Requirements Statement

3. The User Request is the initial approach from the proponent (i.e., the user) for data processing assistance. It contains a brief problem description.

4. The Systems Proposal is essentially a major report resulting from a systems survey. It may be considered as a feasibility report, including a detailed specification of the recommended approach and project plan.

5. The Analytical Report is essentially a project plan, supplemented as necessary with evaluation information.

6. The Design Requirements Statement is essentially a specification of requirements in systems terms.

7. One method of employing these documents is to prepare a User Request and a Systems Proposal. This would be necessary for a major project which required an exhaustive survey and feasibility analysis.

8. An alternative method is to use the User Request and an Analytical Report and/or a Design Requirements Statement.

CHAPTER 4

System Documentation

The systems analysis and design process can be defined in terms of the input documents received and the output documents produced. The systems development process can be said to begin with the production and approval of the final analytical documentation and the authority to proceed with the project. As discussed in the previous chapter, the level and scope of this analytical documentation will depend primarily on the type of project. The major output from the systems development process is a *Systems Specification*. The Systems Specification is the basic medium of communication between the system design function, the programming function and the user. It forms a permanent record of the structure, functions, flow and control of the system. The successful completion of the Systems Specification may be taken as indicating the completion of the systems design process. However, the systems analysis and design personnel will also participate in the system implementation process (e.g., user training, assistance with programming, file conversion, parallel running, etc.).

The production of a document of such scope is of necessity a lengthy process. The level and content of the information is detailed, and the number and type of intended readers many. Thus, the organization of the document and the method of presenting material must be carefully planned. One suggested approach described below is to consider the Systems Specification as comprising a number of documents. This approach requires the production of six sub-set specifications, namely:

- Systems Summary
- File Specifications
- Transaction (Input) Specifications

36

- Output Specifications
- Processing (Program) Specifications
- Systems Test Plan

Each of the above specifications is described below, in terms of content, usage, suggested methods of presentation, and the relationship with the previously produced analytical documentation.

As a general note, however, the size and scope of the Systems Specification are dependent on the type of project development work required. Thus, a major systems revision or completely new system would require a full Systems Specification. However, the production of a new report from existing data sources, or the modification of the physical layout of a file, may only require a concise one- or two-page specification.

As a matter of procedure, however, a standard should be laid down that a formal Systems Specification of some kind must be prepared for all project work. For minor revisions, the Systems Specification may simply be some form of analytical documentation with a few details added. However, to have the positive presentation of a specification with a formal agreement/acceptance procedure establishes a clear "freeze" procedure before the subsequent programming and implementation tasks are undertaken.

SYSTEMS SUMMARY

The Systems Summary is a general description of the complete system or system change. The summary serves three main purposes.

1. To present a non-technical description of the proposed system to non-data processing management to enable them to understand, approve and participate in the system.

2. To present an overall description of the system to show the relationship between the files, inputs, outputs and logical processing steps which are later considered as separate entities.

3. To present specific cross-referenced lists and to define essential terms used in the other specifications.

A sample of a formal table of contents is shown in Figure 4.1. A description of the possible contents is given below and is related for explanatory purposes to the sample table of contents.

Management Summary

The Management Summary should be written in concise non-technical terms for user management. As shown in Figure 4.1, the systems designer is restricted to a logical format of four sub-sections:

SYSTEMS SUMMARY — I

Table of Contents

1.0 Management Summary
    1.1   Purpose and Function
    1.2   Files Maintained and Affected
    1.3   Input and Input Sources
    1.4   Output and Output Uses

2.0 System Flowchart
    2.1   Flowchart
    2.2   Reference Lists

3.0 Narrative Description
    3.1   Definitions
    3.2   System Flow

Figure 4.1   Sample Table of Contents—Systems Summary — I

- Purpose and Function
- Files Maintained and Affected
- Input and Input Sources
- Output and Output Users

It is also good practice to establish a maximum length standard restricting the systems designer to producing a Management Summary of from one to three pages.

The *Purpose and Function* sub-section is used to explain what the system or system changes are intended to accomplish and how these objectives are achieved. In most cases a few sentences only are adequate to explain why a system/system change is necessary and to place it in the context of the working environment.

The *Files Maintained and Affected* sub-section identifies those principal files used in the system and also those files which are affected in other systems. This may be presented by giving a simple summary list showing name, brief definition of content, type of storage medium, and how the file is affected.

The *Input and Input Sources* sub-section may be a summary list, showing input name, brief definition of content and the source (originator) of the input.

The *Output and Output Users* sub-section deals with outputs from the system which are intelligible to the user, i.e., reports and messages rather than magnetic tape or disk files. This again may be a summary list showing name of output, form of output (printed report, typewriter message, visual display, etc.), and who will use the output and how.

Note that if a detailed Design Requirements Statement has been produced during the project initiation and review phase (see page 31), much of the information presented in this section will be a summarization of information given in that report.

System Flowchart

This section is used to present a graphical representation of the overall logic of the system. The System Flowchart should indicate the relationship between each of the logical elements in the system, where a logical element may be considered as a program, off-line machine operation or manual clerical operation (in user or data processing department). Since the flowchart will be supported by various narrative descriptions (sub-sections 2.2 and 3.2 in terms of the sample table of contents, Figure 4.1) the flowchart should simply identify each operation, the data affected in the operation and when the operation takes place.

If any group of systems designers from different working environments were asked to prepare a Systems Flowchart of the same system the result, in terms of layout, symbology and operation descriptions, would differ according to each personal school of thought. For ease of communication and clarity of meaning, localized standards for system flowchart preparation should be established. The main areas for standardization are listed below.

1. Overall layout of flowchart. *Example:*

- the chart must be as clear and simple as possible
- only one line of flow should be shown on a page
- the direction of the flow should be vertical

2. Paging and identification. *Example:*

- within the rule that each major process (e.g., program) must be shown as one symbol, as few pages as possible should be used
- flowcharts should be drawn consistently on a standard size paper
- each page must be identified by system reference (title and number), date of preparation, author identification and page number

3. Symbology. Standard symbols should be established; an example range of standard symbols and their meanings are shown in Appendix B, page 153.

4. Operation (Process) identification/description. *Example:*

- each operation symbol must contain a very brief description of what is accomplished in the operation
- each program run in the system must be clearly labelled with its identification number
- each data element symbol (e.g., file, input or output symbol) should be labelled with the appropriate reference number
- processing cycle (e.g., whether an operation is performed daily, weekly, monthly, as required, etc.), should be clearly indicated on the systems flowchart

The reference number referred to in the third rule above assumes a system in which each file, input and output is assigned a unique identification number. This number indicates the type of data and the reference number with that type—this is explained in more detail later in the chapter.

5. Use of connector symbols. *Example:*

- connector symbols must be used to indicate:
  - (a) off page connections for continuations
  - (b) alternative flow within system
  - (c) interface with other systems
- off page connectors for continuations and alternative flow must indicate the page number and connector identification number of the continuation
- connectors referencing other systems flowcharts should contain the page number and connector identification number of the referenced chart. The system reference number and the date of preparation of the referenced chart should be shown by means of a comment symbol

A sample systems flowchart drawn in accordance with the above rules is shown in Appendix B, page 153.

In some cases, it may be desirable to provide Reference Lists, i.e., summary lists and tables, to support a complex system flowchart. Whereas the system flowchart is logic-flow oriented, reference lists can be, for example, program, file or report oriented. Thus, programs could be listed by frequency and sequence in the processing cycle and files listed by frequency of use and status, again within the processing cycle.

Decision tables (described later in Appendix C, page 167), may be included to support the flowchart. Decision tables will be useful to indicate and explain multiple-flow systems where the processing flow taken at any one time depends on conditions present at time of processing.

Narrative Description

This section comprises two sub-sections: 3.1 Definitions and 3.2 System Flow (see Figure 4.1, page 38).

All terms used in the system which have a special application significance and are essential to its understanding, must be defined in the *Definitions* sub-section. Alternatively, where there is a company glossary of data processing and application area terms, this may be referenced.

System Flow is a narrative description of the processes shown in the System Flowchart. The description should always enhance the understanding of the flow rather than form a simple narrative restatement of what the flowchart shows. The narrative should be cross-referenced to the flowchart. This may be done by placing identification letters or step numbers against the process symbols on the flowchart (or in the margin)

SYSTEMS SUMMARY - II

Table of Contents

1.0 General Information

1.1 Cover Page
1.2 Table of Contents
1.3 Revision Page
1.4 References[1]

2.0 Problem Description

2.1 Definition
2.2 Solution
2.3 Results

3.0 System Description

3.1 Capabilities
3.2 Assumptions
3.3 Limitations[2]
3.4 Restrictions
3.5 System Interface[3]

4.0 Software Environment

4.1 Required Operating System Components
4.2 Interrelationships and Dependencies
4.3 Language Utilization
4.4 Special Software Packages
4.5 Subroutine Library Utilization

5.0 Hardware Environment

5.1 Computer and Peripheral Equipment
5.2 Instruction Set[4]
5.3 Auxiliary Equipment
5.4 Interrelationships and Dependencies

Figure 4.2 Sample Table of Contents—Systems Summary – II

6.0   System Segments

     6.n.1 Function
     6.n.2 Interrelationships
     6.n.3 Language
     6.n.4 Timing and Size Estimates
     6.n.5 Interface

7.0   System Logic

     7.1 Description
     7.2 Flowchart

8.0   Glossaries

     8.1 Mnemonics/Terms
     8.2 Symbols

9.0   Bibliography

Notes

1. Contains administrative information, correspondence, etc.
2. "Limitations" may be taken as being self-imposed constraints and "Restrictions" as environmental constraints.
3. This is the link or interface points with other systems.
4. This contains a list of special equipment capabilities, e.g., special floating-point facilities.

Figure 4.2 (continued)

for reference to paragraphs in the narrative description. Alternatively, each narrative paragraph should be identified by a heading which corresponds to identification in each processing block.

AN ALTERNATIVE APPROACH TO THE SYSTEMS SUMMARY

In some instances, the sample table of contents for the Systems Summary given previously may not be adequate to define a complete system. A very large organization, with a rigid reporting structure and complex systems or hardware/software requirements may require a Systems Summary in greater detail. An alternative table of contents is thus shown in Figure 4.2.

Note that sections 1.0, 2.0, 3.0, 7.0 and 8.0 correspond in content (if not by breakdown) to the Systems Summary presented earlier in this chapter. In addition, however, provision is made for descriptions of hardware and software environment (sections 4.0 and 5.0). Section 6.0, "Systems Segments," presents the system as a number of individual processing segments. Each segment is described briefly and the relationship between each segment defined. In a subsequent set of Processing Specifications, the data and processing requirements for each segment are described in detail.

FILE SPECIFICATIONS

This document is a detailed description of the purpose, contents and organization of a file. Use of a File Specification document generally requires that each file be defined in a File Specification, all File Specifications being included in the Systems Specification. A possible exception to this rule could be where an existing file is to be used in the system; the previously prepared File Specification may be referenced or duplicated in the System Specification.

For the purposes of this book, a file is defined as a series of related records, each identified by a key, which is processed more than once. Information will be required on the file as a whole—such as general organization, storage medium, sources of data, etc. At the next level, the format of a record must be described. At the lowest level each of the constituent data elements comprising a record must be described.

A File Specification comprising this information is essential for communication to the programmer, as a permanent record as to the nature of a file (for subsequent use by other systems, system amendment and system modification). It will also serve as a valuable communication aid to the user by means of a formal review step. For example, an established checkpoint by review of the specification can validate that the file *will* grow by not more than 5% per commercial period—the product code *does* require not less than five characters—the quantity field *can* contain an arithmetically negative quantity and so on.

A suggested table of contents for a File Specification is shown in Figure 4.3. A breakdown of the content, and methods of presenting information, in the File Specification is given below.

File Identification and Characteristics

This comprises two sub-sections: general description and file abstract.

The general description is a brief (one or two paragraph) narrative description of the sources and general functional characteristics of the file. The information that should be included is

- brief (two or three sentence) definition of file contents and purpose
- identification of systems in which file is used
- general statement of the source of data and how the file is generated
- general statement of the updating cycle and retention requirements

The File Abstract is a succinct definition of the physical or technical characteristics of a file in quick reference format. Use of a simple pre-printed form is an ideal method of representing the required information. A sample form is shown in Figure 4.4, and examples of the types of entries are listed below.

Storage Medium and Code

- punched cards/paper tape, magnetic disks/disk packs/cards: ASCII, BCD, EBCDIC

File Organization

- sequential, indexed sequential, controlled sequential, random, serial

Record Type

- fixed length, variable length

Update Cycle

- days in processing cycle when file is brought up-to-date, date from which information in file is valid, reference numbers/titles of programs performing the updating

Current Volume

- number of records in file at present

FILE SPECIFICATION

Standard Table of Contents

1.0 File Identification and Characteristics

    1.1 Genera Description

    1.2 File Abstract

2.0 Record Format

3.0 Data Element Descriptions

4.0 Appendices

    4.1 Record Layouts

    4.2 Edit Lists

    4.3 Cross-Reference Lists

Figure 4.3   Sample Table of Contents—File Specifications

File Abstract Form

File Name _____

File Medium and Code _____

File Organization _____

Record Sequence _____

Header Label _____ Trailer Label _____

Record Type _____ Maximum Length _____

Blocking Factor _____ Maximum Size _____

Update Cycle _____

File Security Classification _____

Current Volume _____ Growth _____

Retention Characteristics _____

_____

_____

Remarks _____

_____

_____

_____

_____

_____

_____

_____

Figure 4.4   Sample File Abstract Form

RECORD FORMAT

File Mnemonic_____ Date _____

Record Type _____

| Relative Positions | | Field Label | Program Mnemonic | Length | Type |
First	Last				

Figure 4.5 Sample Record Format Form

Growth

- rate of increase/decrease/fluctuation in number of records in file, expressed in terms of percentage increase/decrease per unit time, or as specific number of records per unit time

Retention Characteristics

- number of generations maintained, period of retention of generation before purging

A form similar to that shown in Figure 4.4 should provide an adequate technical description of the basic file characteristics.

Record Format

The next section of the File Specification, "Record Format," deals with the record-level information. Again, use of some sort of printed form will aid the presentation of information about record structure, use and content. A sample Record Format form is shown in Figure 4.5. One form is prepared for each record type in the file. The information recorded is defined below.

Relative Position

- this may be specified by the systems designer at the time the document is prepared or, alternatively, it may be completed by the programmer

Field Label

- this is the title given to the data element (and is a means of cross reference to a Data Element Description described later)

Program Mnemonic

- unless a centralized authority assigns mnemonic label for use in the program(s) referencing the data element; this is completed by the programmer

Length

- this defines the length of the data element

Type

- this defines the data element as being numeric, alphabetic, alphanumeric

An alternative system of representation is the use of a free form graphic description similar to the sample shown in Figure 4.6. Note that the

RECORD LAYOUT FORM

Page _____ of _____
Date _____

Record Name _____
Organization _____

DS Name _____
Record Length _____

Field Label

Field Description

Field Usage

Field Label

Field Description

Field Usage

Field Label

Field Description

Field Usage

Field Label

Field Description

Field Usage

Files:

Processes:

Input to:

Output from:

Usage Code

A – Alphanumeric
B – Binary
F – Floating Point
N – Zoned Decimal
P – Packed Decimal

Figure 4.6 Sample Free Form

field usage indicates the type of field (by means of a simple usage code as shown) and its length. For example, an entry A.6 could mean the field comprises six alphanumeric characters.

Data Element Descriptions

Thus far, a method of file descriptive documentation has been presented which has been concerned with the characteristics of the file as a whole and with the composition of records. In the latter case, however, the content of a record was defined purely in terms of the relative position, name, length and type (alphanumeric, etc.) of each data element. As discussed previously, one purpose of the Record Format definition is to act as an index to a number of individual Data Element Description forms, each of which contains all the information required to define a field. The main reason for using this three-level system of file definition is that the same data elements may appear in a number of files (and also in inputs or outputs). Thus, one description of a data element may be prepared and the description cross referenced whenever necessary. Further, there may even be a case in some installations for establishing a central control point for the approval/assignment of data element name. Again, use of a pre-printed form may prove worthwhile to discipline the systems designer in presenting specific information about a data element in a standard manner. A sample form is shown in Figure 4.7; description of the contents is given below.

The form is headed with the Field Label (cross referenced from the Record Format), the file name or mnemonic, the date and the author's name. A short description of the data element and source is then given, followed by the definition of length, format and values. In some cases, a field may be defined for future use; i.e. space is provided for a field in a file but at the time the field is defined, it has no processing significance. Thus, provision is made for stating a "reserved" category and defining the present contents of the field. For example, under the Reserved heading may be "for future use" and the entry under Contents may read "filler 9's".

Similarly, some organizations employ a security classification system which defines the levels and methods for personnel to access information held in certain data elements. Thus, the contents of a field may be "scrambled" and only certain approved personnel given the means to interpret the information. On the sample form shown, provision is made for recording the security classification. Under "Addenda" any other relevant information for the understanding of the data element is entered. The information recorded should include such items as:

DATA ELEMENT DESCRIPTION

Field Label _____

Group Label _____

File Mnemonic _____   Date _____

Description _____

_____

Length & Form _____

Values _____

_____

Reserved _____   Contents _____

Security Classification _____

Source _____

Addenda _____

_____

_____

_____

Figure 4.7   Sample Data Element Description Form

- scaling factor
- description or reference to coding system employed
- units of measure

Appendices

The remainder of the File Specification, the "Appendices," can be used to record additional optional information which will assist in use of the specification. Examples of possible appendices are

- record layouts: graphical representations of tape, disk or card record layouts
- edit lists: tabular representation of editing criteria for acceptable and unacceptable conditions and values of various data elements in a file
- cross reference lists: various lists produced as required, which may include index to data elements, reference list showing which transactions produce which file data, and summary tables showing the frequency and use of files within a system

TRANSACTION (INPUT) SPECIFICATIONS

This document describes all the inputs to the system. For the purposes of this book, a transaction is defined as an input which generates some activity in the system, e.g., changes to a file. In addition, the Input Specification describes these transactions in the form in which they enter the computer system, not as they appear at some earlier or later stage of their processing.

For example, if a source document is entered into the computer processing system, the information punched in cards and the contents of the cards written onto magnetic tape (to form, say, a daily order file), the punched card form of the transaction is then described in the Input Specification.

A sample table of contents for an Input Specification is shown in Figure 4.8; the contents and methods of presenting information are discussed below.

Identification

This simply identifies the report by referencing the system, author and date of preparation.

INPUT SPECIFICATION

Standard Table of Contents

1.0   Identification

2.0   Transaction Listing

3.0   Input Layouts and Samples

Figure 4.8   Sample Table of Contents—Input Specification

Transaction Listing

A Transaction Listing is a convenient method of summarizing the characteristics of all inputs to the system. As in the File Specification report, pre-printed forms or predefined formats may be used to discipline the systems designer to present the required information in a standard manner. A sample form is shown in Figure 4.9 and its contents discussed below.

Transaction Title

- an assigned short name identifying the transaction; if a transaction coding system is used, the transaction identification number may be specified here

Media and Identification

- the media on which the transaction is recorded is stated (e.g., magnetic tape, punched card or paper tape, etc.), together with the identifying name of the media and transaction. For example, the media identification for a punched card transaction would be the card format; however, one card format may hold a number of different transaction types, and thus the particular card-type code must be specified for each transaction type

Purpose

- a brief statement of the purpose served by the input in a system

Affects

- this should show the program name/number(s) of the program(s) which process the transaction, and a reference to the files that are changed by the transaction

Frequency

- this states the processing cycle of the transaction, i.e. the frequency with which the input will enter the system

Volume

- an estimate of approximate volume of this transaction type

Source

- a reference to the originating source of the transaction

Transaction Description

The Transaction Listing identifies and presents a general description of all inputs to the system. The Transaction Description, however, presents

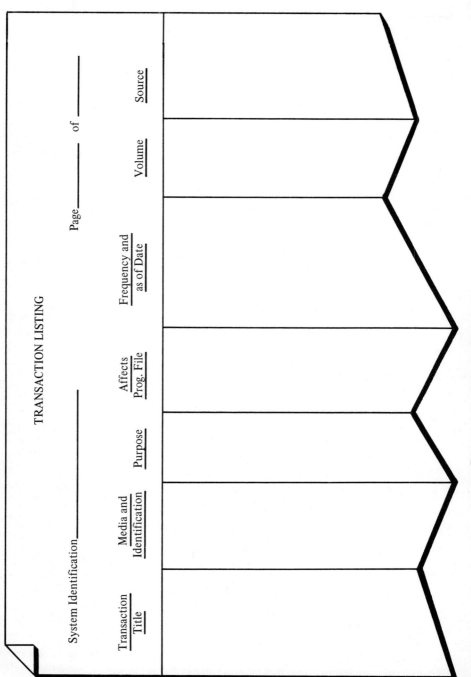

Figure 4.9   Sample Transaction Listing

a detailed description of the contents of each input. A sample pre-printed form is shown in Figure 4.10; use of this form requires that each input be described on one form. An explanation of the content is given below.

Field Label

- an assigned name to identify the field

Field Length and Type

- this defines the length of the field and the type (e.g., numeric, alphabetic, binary, etc.)

Values

- the range of values (minimum and maximum, special conditions) that the field may hold

Edit Criteria

- this is a summary of the acceptable and unacceptable data conditions and values for entering the system. The acceptable conditions and values should be listed first, followed by the unacceptable ones. The latter should be accompanied by a statement of required action for each unacceptable condition

Note that a system of Data Element Descriptions as described on page 51 may be used to supplement or replace part of the Transaction Description.

Input Layouts and Samples

This section should list the input formats to be used in the system. Each format should be documented by showing

- a layout; in rough form or final copy
- a reference list of transactions to layout
- samples of filled-out formats

The samples need only be included if they will aid the understanding of the input.

OUTPUT SPECIFICATIONS

The Output Specification details the systems outputs—why and when produced, contents, formats and recipients. By output is meant here any product of the system which is to be used elsewhere. Thus, under this definition, messages to equipment operators and intermediate files (inter-

Transaction Description

Transaction Name _____

Relative Position	Field Label	Field Length and Type	Values	Edit Criteria

Figure 4.10   Sample Transaction Description

facing two or more segments in the same system) are excluded from the Output Specification. The Specification does include descriptions of such material as reports, messages to remote terminals, output, magnetic and paper tape for input to a data transmission process. A sample table of contents is shown in Figure 4.11. Note that the method of treatment is similar to Input Specification, i.e., outputs are listed, formats shown and the individual data elements defined.

Identification

This simply identifies the output by referencing the system, the author and the date of preparation.

Output Listing

This is a list of all outputs from the system in the general sequence in which they are produced. For each output, the following information is given (possibly on a pre-printed form as shown in Figure 4.12).

Output Name

- the assigned name of the output and possibly a reference number; where a number of output types are produced, such as a number of message types, classed as one output, each output type is defined

Program Number

- the reference number of the program generating the output

Media and Media Identification

- the type of output media (printed reports, punched cards, magnetic tape, etc.) and the output media identification number or symbol (label or card number, etc.)

Purpose

- the purpose and content are briefly summarized

Frequency and Volume

- this defines the day or date in the processing cycle when the report is produced; the approximate volume should be shown in the appropriate unit of measurement

Number of Copies (Distribution) and Destination

- for a printed report, the number of copies should be specified and a distribution list given; for other outputs, the destination should be specified; e.g., the system reference and point of entry for an output magnetic tape file

OUTPUT SPECIFICATION

Standard Table of Contents

1.0   Identification

2.0   Output Listing

3.0   Output Description

4.0   Output Formats

Figure 4.11 Sample Table of Contents—Output Specification

Output Listing

System Identification _____

Output Name	Program No.	Media and Media Identification	Purpose	Frequency and Volume	No. of Copies and Destination

Figure 4.12   Sample Output Listing

Output Description

Having defined the general characteristics of the output in the Output Listing, the detailed contents of each output are defined in the Output Description. An Output Description is prepared for each output of the system: a sample pre-printed form is shown in Figure 4.13. The entries are described below.

Positions

- the positions occupied on the output file report or message. Where the exact format of a message card or tape output has not been formalized, the relative position may be stated

Field Label

- the assigned name of the field

Source

- the source of a data element in a field is specified (i.e., cross referenced to a specific input data element or file data element)

Length and Format

- the length and format of field are defined, e.g., number of characters and edit requirements—position of sign, currency symbol, decimal point, zero suppression requirements etc.

Program

- the program reference number of the program generating the output

Note that the Output Description describes only data fields: indicative data such as printed headings, etc., should be shown on output formats. Again, a series of Data Element Descriptions may be used as described on page 51, to describe the contents of fields.

Output Formats

Samples of output should be included in the form of layouts or copies, keyed to names and/or numbers in the Output Listing. Report formats would customarily be finalized at the system design stage. However, in some organizations precise formats of messages, card or tape layouts may be omitted if these have not been defined at the design stage. When report layouts are shown, standards should be laid down for their presentation. For example, the difference of printed and preprinted heading should be apparent, layouts should be drawn on a standard form, sample

Output Description

Output Name _____

Positions	Field Label	Source	Length and Format	Program	Layout Reference

Figure 4.13   Sample Output Description

values should be included showing minimum/maximum/special values and so on.

PROCESSING (PROGRAM) SPECIFICATIONS

In the method of system documentation used as an example in this chapter, a Program Specification comprises the File, Input and Output Specifications, and a Processing Specification.

The Processing Specification is essentially a statement of the design requirements and general logic for a program. It is prepared by the systems designer (possibly with assistance from the programming function) to enable the programmer to develop processing logic. One Processing Specification is thus prepared for each program. Note, however, that in a complex system as defined by means of the detailed Systems Summary on page 37, the *segment* concept of processing may be used. In this case, each major logical segment of the system may be described by a Segment Processing Specification. This specification may encompass a number of programs. For ease of documentation, this specification should be broken down into a number of Processing Specifications. This then gives the required one Processing Specification per program.

The Processing Specification may either be "free form" within a laid-down table of contents or may be based on a pre-printed form with standard headings. Irrespective of the format, the information listed below must be given. Secondly, to obviate unnecessary duplication, the information must be presented in a form such that it can readily be incorporated (as introductory material) in the program documentation. Information requirements are:

- the inputs to a program,
- the outputs of a program,
- the major functions performed,
- the means of communication between this program and previous/following programs,
- the logical rules and decisions to be followed (defined in decision tables if necessary), including a statement of how the input is to be examined, altered and utilized,
- the validation and edit criteria,
- the action to be taken on error or exception conditions,
- special tables, formulas, and algorithms, and
- the parameters to be entered if a utility program is to be used, e.g., sort sequence and keys for a sort program.

One method of presenting the above information is by using a pre-printed form similar to that sample shown in Figure 4.14. The form is completed according to the following three rules:

1. Define each file and input to the program by

    - showing the appropriate input/file symbol and connecting it to the input line
    - entering into the symbol the appropriate file name and identification number
    - drawing a connector symbol above the input/file symbol, and stating the origin of that input/file in the symbol

2. Define each output and file produced by the program by

    - drawing the appropriate output/file symbol and connecting it to the output line
    - entering into the symbol the appropriate output/file name and identification number
    - drawing a connector symbol below the output/file symbol and stating the destination of that output/file in the symbol stated

3. In the processing box, enter the purpose and function of the program, and refer to supplementary sheets giving the additional material.

SYSTEMS TEST PLAN

The Systems Test Plan is a permanent record of the testing procedure to prove the system prepared by the systems design function. Note that it is distinct from the program test plan which includes a series of test cases prepared by a programmer to prove a program.

The Systems Test Plan should

- explain the purpose of the test designs
- define test inputs and files
- specify test procedures
- define outputs to be achieved

Thus, the test plan establishes the requirements to be met before the system can be considered as being operational.

A sample table of contents is shown in Figure 4.15.

Identification

This references the System Specification of which the test plan is a part.

PROCESSING SPECIFICATION

System _____ Program _____

Prepared by _____ Date _____

(Inputs and Files)

Processing

(Outputs and Files)

Figure 4.14   Sample Processing Specification

SYSTEMS TEST PLAN

Table of Contents

1.0 Identification

2.0 Test Organization

3.0 Validity Criteria

    3.1 Control

    3.2 Processing

    3.3 Output

4.0 Test Schedule

5.0 Test Cases

    5.1 Test Case 1

    5.2 Test Case n

Figure 4.15 Sample Table of Contents—Systems Test Plan

Test Organization

This summarizes

- test objectives for the system
- responsibility allocation for conducting the tests, for coordination with runs and data sources, and for maintenance of the test material
- references to other systems which have provided tests of some components of this system; e.g., existing files and inputs previously tested for another system

Validity Criteria

This section may be considered as comprising a "quality control" specification for data and procedures. It is a description of the test criteria for all conditions in the system. These conditions include: control, processing and output test criteria.

Control conditions include criteria for such functions as

- permissible error tolerances
- provision of check points for error recovery
- pre-processing requirements
- acceptance of files and file records
- acceptance of input

Processing criteria should be included for such functions as

- valid and invalid combinations of input and file data
- invalid codes and code combinations
- invalid parameter options

Output criteria should be shown for such conditions as

- message length and format
- output designations and codes
- report spacing limits

Test Schedule

This section lists the sequence of operations for performing a complete systems test. The steps required and the appropriate sequence can be defined by means of a standard preprinted form similar to the sample shown in Figure 4.16. The required information is summarized below. Step Number

- all operations in the test are assigned a number to indicate the sequence in which the tests are applied

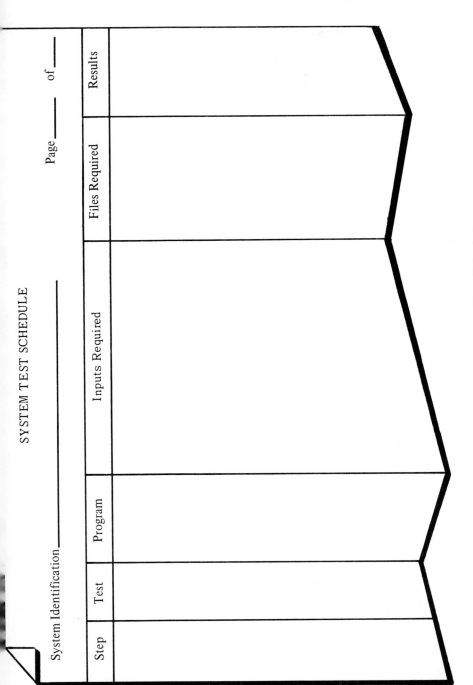

SYSTEM TEST SCHEDULE

Page ——— of ———

System Identification ———

Step	Test	Program	Inputs Required	Files Required	Results

Figure 4.16   Sample Systems Test Schedule

Test Number

- all test cases are assigned an identification number

Program Number

- the program involved in this step

Input Required

- the inputs required for a test are listed here by input name (and/or reference number); the source and date of the test data should also be shown (e.g., whether the data is artificial test data or selected live cases)

Files Required

- the files required for a test are listed here by file name (and/or reference number); the source and date of the file data should be identified (e.g., whether the data is artificial or live)

Results

- the desired results for each step in the systems test should be stated; this may be by reference to the documented test cases as defined below

Test Cases

Each test case should be described in a sub-section and the sub-section identified by the test number. For each test case, the test inputs, files and outputs should be defined.

A Test File should be explained in terms of

- organization and contents of the file
- test file data identification and printout of files permanently maintained for test file purposes.

Test Inputs should be defined in terms of content by transaction type. Permanently maintained test inputs should be shown by layout or print out.

Test Outputs should show a sample of each derived output from each step in which the test case is involved.

Test files and input descriptions should include a statement of the purpose of the data, i.e., the section criteria for a transaction type of test file records. Test outputs should state what is being tested in the production of each output.

COMPOSITE DESCRIPTIVE FORMS

The file, input and output documentation described previously in this Chapter used a technique of Data Element Description forms. This technique gave a modular approach to documentation and, by having separate descriptions of data elements, it obviates the need for including a description of the same data element in every file, input type or output type containing that element.

This part of the chapter presents an alternative approach. Essentially, this approach attempts to use one basic form to record all the information to file, input and output. There is, of course, the sheer practicality of designing a form of usable physical size. However, if an overflow occurs, additional information is appended and cross referenced to the form.

Input Forms

A sample input form is shown in Exhibit 4.17. The circled numbers shown in Figure 4.17 are cross-referenced to Figure 4.18 which describes the entries. Note that the form shows:

 Identification Data
 Field Content Data
 Statistical Information
 Retention and Security Requirements
 Input Preparation Requirements

SUMMARY

 1. The basic output from the systems analysis and design phase should be a System Specification.
 2. The System Specification is the definition of the system in terms of its functions, scope, flow and controls.
 3. A suggested approach to the preparation of a Systems Specification is the preparation of a multi-section document comprised of

- Systems Summary
- File Specifications
- Transaction Specifications
- Output Specifications
- Processing Specifications
- Systems Test Plan

Input Origin			
Record Name	⑤		
From (Title/Dept)	⑥		
Frequency	⑦		
Take-on volumes (average/peak)	⑧		
Normal volumes (average/peak)	⑨		
Record size (average/max)	⑩		
Input Medium/Device	⑪		
Conversion method	⑫		
Code	⑬		

File Size		
Number	Take-on	Normal
of Ave		
Records Peak		
Record Size Ave		
Peak		
% Hit Rate		
% Change		
% Growth		

File Sequence	
Major	
Key Fields	⑭
Minor	

Cycling & Security Procedures
⑮

Programs using File			
Program No.	R_W	Program No.	R_W
		⑯	

File Description	
Prepared by ⑰ Approved by	

Position	Correlation	Level	Field Co Names
⑲	⑱	⑳	㉑

Figure 4.17   Sample Input Description Form

File Storage Details			Identification	
Medium			File No.	①
Number of volumes			File Title	②
			Page No.	of
Device model no.			Brief Description	③
Number of drives				
Blocking factor			Date	④

FIELD DESCRIPTION

rmat Size	Bytes Words	Occur	V	Ldg Zero	Sign	Further Description (including details of validity checks to be applied on input).
㉒	㉓	㉔	㉕	㉖	㉗	㉘

CIRCLED ENTRIES ON FIGURE 4.17

1   A local code which is a unique number assigned to the input.

2   A brief English language title of the input.

3   A brief description of the input in non-technical terms.

4   The date on which the Input Description Form was completed.

5   The record name identifying each record name.

6   The source of the record type, specified by either title of person or department originating the input. Names of persons must not be used.

7   The frequency at which the record type is processed (e.g., daily or weekly).

8   The volume of input records that must initially be processed during the conversion process to the new system.

9   The estimated volume of input records during actual system running. It is the number of records per day, week or period, etc. as specified under "Frequency."

10   The size of the record specifying the maximum and, for variable length records, average record size.

11   The medium used for the input, e.g., paper tape, encoded document, transmission keyboard, must be entered here.

12   The means by which the input is converted to a machine-sensible form.

13   The code (e.g., card or paper punching code) of the input medium.

14   Where the input is required to be in a particular sequence the sort key fields must be specified in this box. In other cases the word "RANDOM" must be specified.

15   The retention time and manner of authorization for disposal of the source documents (if any) or coded input media.

16   The numbers of all programs using the input.

17   The signatures of systems designer and/or job analyst.

18   This column may be used for correlation purposes, e.g., to indicate the untimate use of the data.

19   The position of the start of the data element in a record specified by column number or character.

20   The level number as described on page 76.

21   The COBOL (or other preferred language) name for the date element should be entered in this column. The name should not be more than 8 characters.

22   A code is entered in this column to indicate the format and size of the data item. The codes used are:

Figure 4.18   Summary of Contents of Input Description Form

CIRCLED ENTRIES ON FIGURE 4.17

(22)
A — alphanumeric (characters)

B — binary (bits)

C — packed decimal (digits)

D — decimal (digits)

E — long precision floating point (double words)

F — short precision floating point (words)

P — PICTURE

The code is followed by a number in brackets indicating the number of digits or characters. Decimal or binary codes may be followed by two numbers separated by a period: the second number indicates the number of digits following the assumed decimal or binary point. Examples of the codes are:

A (25) — a 25 character alphnumeric field

B (32) — a 32 bit binary number

C (8.2) — a 10 digit packed dec decimal number including 2 digits to the right of the decimal point

D (5) — a 5 digit unpacked decimal number

The code P is used for data whose format cannot easily be described with the codes above. Following the P any valid COBOL or LP1 picture may be written enclosed in quotation marks.

23 This field is not applicable for prime input descriptions.

24 This column must be completed for any data field which may occur more than once. The maximum number of occurences is entered.

25 The letter 'V' is entered in this column if the number of occurences is variable.

26 Presence of leading zeros exist in the input field.

27 A code should be entered to indicate the existence and position of an operational sign. A suggested code is:

L — sign in left hand digit position

LO — sign as overpunch in left hand digit position

R — sign as right hand digit position

RO — sign as overpunch in right hand digit position

NS — not signed

28 Any other relevant information may be written in this column.

Figure 4.18 (continued)

The contents of the above were discussed.

Note that the structure of the form is as follows:

Circled Nos. in Fig. 4.17	*Entries*
1 to 4	Basic identification.
5 to 13	Descriptions of the origination and preparation of the input, and record size, frequency and volume data. Each input type is assigned a record name (5), and entries 6 to 13 in a vertical column are completed for each input type.
14 and 15	The sequence of the input (if any) and the retention requirements for original documents and media.
16	A list of those programs which use the prime input.
17	Housekeeping entries recording, by signature, the persons who have prepared and approved the form.
18 to 28	These columns are used to identify each data element (e.g., record and field) existing in an input. Entries must be made according to a COBOL type level structure where level 01 corresponds to a record. If more than one type of record exists in an input, each record type should be shown. Record descriptions should be separated by a bold horizontal line.

The Input Description form may be supplemented by sample layouts. When designing cards and documents for input to the computer system it must always be remembered that one of the aims of the computer based data processing is to eliminate tedious clerical procedures. Layouts should always be designed firstly for ease of use completion, secondly for ease of punching and lastly for ease of processing.

The layout of input medium should be drawn on card layouts or file layout forms supplied by the manufacturer. A similar system may be employed for file and output descriptions, as described below.

File Description Forms

This form, supplemented where necessary by additional narrative, will be the major source of reference for

Users
Programmers
Operations Personnel

The *File Description Form,* Figure 4.19, is the definitive description of a file. The form is comprised of

Identification Data
Field Content Data
Statistical Information (sizes, hit rate, volumes, etc.)
File Storage Device Characteristics
Cycling and Security Requirements

In circumstances where insufficient space is provided on the form, cross-references may be made on the form to supplementary sheets. The general arrangement of a completed form is as follows.

Circled Nos. *in Fig. 4.19*	*Entries*
1 to 4	Basic identification entries.
5 to 9	Definition of the file storage device to be used.
10 to 15	File size and hit rate statistics, and file sequence.
16	Cycling and security requirements for the file.
17	List of programs which use the file.
18	Housekeeping entries, recording by signature, the persons who have prepared and approved the form.
19 to 29	These columns are used to identify each data element (e.g., record and field) in a file. Entries must be made according to a COBOL type level structure where level 01 corresponds to a record. If more than one type of record exists in a file, each record type should be shown. Record descriptions should be separated by a bold horizontal line.

Figure 4.20 summarizes the contents of the form.

In addition to the specification of the file on the File Description Form, a detailed layout of the file must be shown on a File Layout Form. Suitable forms for this purpose are provided by the computer manufacturers. The layout must include labels, tape marks and any special software data fields, such as block length records, as well as all the data fields. Where a file is held on a direct access device, a File Map should be prepared to define the layout of the file on a device, e.g., the start/end limits of the file, the index areas and the overflow areas.

Output Forms

All reports produced in a system are defined by means of a

- Report Description Form
- Report Layout
- Report Production Form.

Input Origin

Record Name			
From (Title/Dept)			
Frequency			
Take-on volumes (average/peak)			
Normal volumes (average/peak)			
Record size (average/max)			
Input Medium/Device			
Conversion method			
Code			

File Size

Number	Take-on	Normal
of Ave		
Records Peak	⑩	
Record Size Ave		
Peak	⑪	
% Hit Rate	⑫	
% Change	⑬	
% Growth	⑭	

File Sequence

Key Fields Major	
Minor	⑮

Cycling & Security Procedures

⑯

Programs using File

Program No.	R_W	Program No.	R_W
		⑰	

File Description

Prepared by   ⑱   Approved by

Position	Correlation	Level	Field Code Names
⑲	⑳		㉒

Figure 4.19   Sample File Description Form ►

File Storage Details	
Medium	⑤
Number of volumes	⑥
Device model no.	⑦
Number of drives	⑧
Blocking factor	⑨

Identification	
File No.	①
File Title	②
Page No.	of
Brief Description	③
Date	④

FIELD DESCRIPTION

rmat Size	Bytes Words	Occur	V	Ldg Zero	Sign	Further Description (including details of validity checks to be applied on input).
㉓	㉔	㉕	㉖	㉗	㉘	㉙

CIRCLED ENTRIES ON FIGURE 4.19

1 A unique file identification number assigned to the file.

2 A brief English language title of the file

3 A brief description of the file in non-technical terms.

4 The date on which the File Description Form was completed.

5 The file storage medium, e.g., disc or tape.

6 This is the estimated number of volumes (discs or tapes) used to hold the file. Where the file size

7 is variable, minimum and maximum figures should be given.

7 The device model number on which the file is to be held.

8 The number of drives that must be allocated to the file when it is held on-line.

9 The blocking factor for the file when stored on the stated device.

10 The number of records in the file under average and peak conditions. The number of records at file take-on (i.e., file conversion) and at normal run time must be stated.

11 The record size defined in characters or words. Fixed length record sizes must be entered under 'MAX' and an 'F' must be written under 'AVE'.

12 The percentage of records in the file that are matched by input records during run. This should be shown by record type within program.

13 This is the rate of change of indicative information on the file over a specified period of time. For example, "20% per month" indicates that 20% of the records are amended by applying new indicative information in a month.

14 This is the net growth rate of the file (total number of records added—number of replaced deletions) as a percentage of total number of records over a specified period of time.

15 Where the file is required to be in a particular sequence, the sort key fields must be specified in this box. In other cases, 'RANDOM' should be specified. Where the file may be held in more than one sequence, the sequence required for each program should be specified.

16 The cycling procedure and security requirements for this file.

17 A list of all programs using the file, stating whether it is read and/or written.

18 The signature of systems designer and/or job analyst.

19 This column may be used for correlation purposes, e.g., to indicate the ultimate use of the data.

20 The position of the start of the data element in a record specified by character position.

21 This is the level number in text.

Figure 4.20   Summary of Contents of File Description Form

CIRCLED ENTRIES ON FIGURE 4.19

22 The COBOL (or other preferred language) name for the data element should be entered in this column. The name should not be more than 8 characters.

23 A code is entered in this column to indicate the format and size of the data item. The codes used are:

A − alphanumeric (characters)

B − binary (bits)

C − packed decimal (digits)

D − decimal (digits)

E − long precision floating point (double words)

F − short precision floating point (words)

P − PICTURE

The code is followed by a number in brackets indicating the number of digits or characters. Decimal or binary codes may be followed by two numbers separated by a period; the second number indicates the number of digits following the assumed decimal or binary point. Examples of the codes are:

A (25) − a 25 character a alphanumeric field

B (32) − a 32 bit binary number

C (8.2) − a 10 digit packed decimal number including 2 digits to the right of the decimal point

D (5) − a 5 digit unpacked decimal number

The code P is used for data whose format cannot easily be described with the codes above. Following the P any valid COBOL or PL1 picture may be written enclosed in quotation marks.

24 In cases where the number of bytes (IBM 360) or words (ICT 1900) to be occupied by the data field is not clear from the 'Format and Size' entry, the size in words or bytes should be stated here.

25 This column must be completed for any data field which may occur more than once. The maximum number of occurances is entered.

26 The letter 'V' is entered in this co column if the number of occurences is varaible.

27 The presence of leading zeros in the field.

28 A code should be entered here to indicate the existence and position of an operational sign. A suggested code is:

28

A (25) − a 25 character alphanumeric field

B (32) − a 32 bit binary number

C (8.2) − a 10 digit packed decimal number including 2 digits to the right of the decimal point

D (5) − a 5 digit unpacked decimal number

29 Any other relevant information may be written in this column.

Figure 4.20 (continued)

Report Size		
	Normal	Peak
Lines or Pages	(8)	

Report Sequence
(9)

Distribution Instructions (10)

	Special Instructions	
Send to	Dept.	
	Title	
Other		
Photocopy		
Microfilm		
Guillotine		
Strip		
Decollate		
Burst		
Copy		

Print Positions	Source	Level
		01
(11)	(12)	(13)

Report Description	
Prepared by (18)	Approved by

Figure 4.21   Sample Report Description Form

SCRIPTION FORM

Format Information		
aty · Type	⑦	
ormat ape No.	⑥	
age umbering ystem	⑤	

Identification		
Report No.	①	
Title	②	
Page No.	of	
Brief Description	③	
Date	④	

FIELD DESCRIPTION			
de	Format & Size	Editing Requirements	Further Description
	⑮	⑯	⑰

The Report Description Form defines the relevant data elements, distribution data, report sequence and size. The Report Layout is an example of the printed form. The Report Production Form specifies the conditions under which records (lines) are printed, spacing between lines and so on. These documents will be the basis for the communication of information about the report to the users, programmers and operations personnel.

Each report produced in a system must be defined by means of a *Report Description Form,* as shown in Figure 4.21. The report comprises

- Identification Data
- Field Content Data
- Distribution Instructions
- Report Size and Sequence Information.

Where there is insufficient space on the form, cross references may be made on the form to supplementary sheets. The main part of the form is a Field Description (circled numbers 11 to 17, Figure 4.21). These columns are used to identify each data element existing in a report. Entries must be made according to a COBOL type level structure where level 01 corresponds to a record. If more than one record type exists in an output, each record type should be shown. Record descriptions should be separated by a bold horizontal line.

Figure 4.22 gives brief notes on individual entries on the form.

A detailed layout of each report must be drawn on a *Report Layout* sheet as supplied by the manufacturer. If the report is to be printed on pre-printed stationery, a sample of the form should be attached to the layout sheet and the pre-printed portion pasted over the layout sheet. Information which results from processing should be indicated by X's written in the appropriate print position. The maximum field sizes for variable data should be shown. Constant information, such as headings, fixed signs, etc. should be printed neatly in the required print positions.

A *Report Production Form* as shown in Figure 4.23, must be completed for each report. For each record (i.e., line) defined by a level 01 entry on the Report Description Form, this schedule specifies the conditions governing the production of the record and the vertical spacing required before printing it.

4. The contents of the File, Transaction and Output Specifications were discussed in terms of a free form or pre-printed form approach. The use of a three level document system was suggested in which

- level one was an overall description of the file, or list of transactions or outputs
- level two was a description of the format and overall content of a file, transaction or output record
- level three was a Data Element Description which described the format, contents and use of each field

CIRCLED ENTRIES ON FIGURE 4.21

1   A unique report identification number.

2   A brief English language title of the report.

3   A brief description of the report in non-technical terms.

4   The date on which the Report Description Form was prepared.

5   The page numbering method required on the report.

6,7 The stationery type and format tape numbers as defined by local standards.

8   The anticipated size of the report in lines and/or pages.

9   The sequence in which the records are printed.

10 Distribution instructions should be entered here.

11 This column is used to specify where on the line the data is to be printed.

12 The source of the data should be stated here. The entry should show whether the data field is taken directly from an input or a file, or is the result of calculation. The name of the file or input and record should be stated. For example, F-SC121M MFSTK INV indicates that the data comes direct from the record called MFSTKINV on file SC 121 M.

13 The COBOL (or other preferred language) name for the data element should be entered in this column. The name should not be more than 8 characters.

14 This the level number as previous in text.

15 A code is entered in this column to indicate the format and size of the data item. The codes used are:

A – alphanumeric (characters)

B – binary (bits)

C – packed decimal (digits)

D – decimal (digits)

E – long precision floating point (double words)

F – short precision floating point (words)

The code is followed by a number in brackets indicating the number of digits or characters. Decimal or binary codes may be followed by two numbers separated by a period; the second number indicates the number of digits following the assumed decimal or binary point. Examples of the codes are:

A (25) – a 25 character alphanumeric field

B (32) – a 32 bit binary number

C (8.2) – a 10 digit packed decimal number including 2 digits to the right of the decimal point

D (5) – a digit unpacked decimal number

The code P is used for data whose format cannot easily be described with the codes above. Following the P any valid COBOL or PL1 picture may be written enclosed in quotation marks.

16 The systems disigner must specify the editing requirements in detail. Items to be specified may include:

zero suppresion,

insertion of punctuation symbols,

insertion of currency symbols, and

cheque protection characters.

17 This column is used for any other information.

18 The signature of the systems designer and/or job analyst.

Figure 4.22   Summary of Contents of Report Description Form

REPORT PRODUCTION FORM

Form Prepared by............................   Report Number.....................

Date............................

Record Name	Conditions governing the production of this report line.	Spacing before this line	
		Normal	H.O.F.

Figure 4.23   Sample Report Production Form

CHAPTER 5

Program Documentation

The limits and responsibilities of the programming function are perhaps the easiest to define in terms of a start and end point. The programming function can be said to commence with the provision of a problem definition and solution specification. From this initial input, detailed program logic is designed, and the program coded and tested. The output is thus a proved and documented program ready for operation, although probably it will be operated initially under a test environment.

Within this simple functional definition, there is a wide range of applicational differences. At one end of the spectrum are the scientific/engineering problem-solving applications in which one man determines that a problem exists, defines the problem, and prepares a solution-giving program. The program may well serve a one-time purpose, the input and file data may be generated solely by the problem originator and the output may be examined and interpreted by the user alone. In such instances there may be one nebulous documenting step from "back-of-envelope jottings" to proved object program listing.

At the other end of this application-type spectrum, the input to the programming function may be a detailed Systems Specification, comprising a number of Program Specifications describing a complex business data processing system. The programming tasks in such a case will be performed by many programmers, possibly with the use of outside contractors. Since communication becomes much more of a problem under such conditions, this chapter is primarily concerned with business data processing programming. Further, it assumes as a starting point the provision of a Systems Specification comprising a number of

Program Specifications with the level of content described in the previous chapter.

The first part of this chapter is concerned principally with application programming; some notes at the end of this chapter are given on software development documentation.

PROGRAMMING—TASKS AND COMMUNICATION

Historically, the tasks of the programming function have usually been the most clearly defined of all the data processing functions. The actual personnel assignment of the tasks however is still the subject of much debate. The recognized programming tasks are

- Logic analysis
- Coding
- Desk checking
- Test data preparation
- Assembly/compilation and testing
- Specification of operating requirements
- Final documentation
- Installation

Associated with these clearly defined tasks is a traditional concept of types and levels of documentation, and agreed lines of communication. These may be stated by briefly reviewing the aims of program documentation. The results of the first five tasks in the above list must be recorded so that

- a change in programmer task assignment may be effected with the minimum of disruption,
- program modifications and corrections may be made efficiently and effectively,
- conversion may be made to new equipment,
- management can assess the progress and quality of the work performed, and
- the programs may be turned over to operations for day-to-day running and maintenance.

From the above, it can be seen that the two main users of program documentation will be programmers and data processing management. Operations will also be a prime user of that part of the program documentation relating to computer operating instructions. These will form part of the total program documentation but will be discussed in greater detail in Chapter 6, *Operations Documentation*. Note, however, that computer or program operating instructions form only a part of the required operating documentation (with data preparation, auxiliary equipment, output dispersal instructions, etc.).

Users may also reference program documentation. However, in a commercial environment, users in the operating departments will generally be more interested in the general program description and in the Program Specification.

Given the above programming tasks and documentation requirements, what is the minimum level of program documentation?

THE PROGRAM MANUAL—THE TRADITIONAL APPROACH

The term Program Manual is used in this book to describe the complete final documentation of a program. The *Traditional Approach* quoted in the title of this section refers to a technique of program documentation which has come to be accepted as an "industry standard" over the past few years. In some instances, it is still a valid approach. It thus forms an excellent starting point for a detailed discussion of program documentation. As we shall see in the next section however, the changing techniques and environment of programming requires in many instances that a different structure and level of program documentation be used.

The Program Manual should contain (or reference)

- a general description of the function, use and methodology of the program,
- descriptions of input, files and output used or produced by the program,
- flow diagrams showing the logic of the program,
- descriptions of instructive output messages (e.g., output on console or printer),
- coding information, e.g., an assembly listing, memory print, descriptions of matrices or tables used,
- test plan, and
- program test and operating instructions.

The content and method of presentation of the above are discussed below in terms of the traditional methods of pure narrative description and flowcharts. The description also assumes original development, i.e. a Program Specification without the elaborate use of application packages or software routines. Alternative methods of representation, the impact of application packages and use of standard software will be discussed later in this chapter.

A sample table of contents for a Program Manual is shown in Figure 5.1.

Identification

Each Program Manual should be identified by at least a system reference (name and number), a program reference (name and number), the author's name, position and location, and the issue date.

Program Description

As shown in Figure 5.1, this can be considered as comprising two sub-sections: a Processing Specification and a description of Program Methodology.

The Processing Specification corresponds to the section in the Programming Specification (described on page 64) prepared by the systems designer. If a Programming Specification is prepared as described in the previous chapter, the Processing Specification may be extracted for inclusion in the Program Manual.

The Programming Methodology sub-section is usually prepared by the programmer, although sufficient information may have been given in the Processing Specification as to make this sub-section unnecessary. Essentially, Program Methodology records, in brief terms, the programmer's approach to the Processing Specification.
This is done by recording such information as

- general logic
- equipment configuration requirements and restraints (special features required, core storage required, etc.)
- subroutines called and their calling sequence
- special formulae used
- any other information of a specialized nature which is not recorded elsewhere

Data Specifications

The file, input and output specifications as described (pages 44–64) should be included. If the finalizing of layouts is the task of the programming function, layouts and samples (if available) should be included.

Program Logic

Traditionally, program logic is represented by means of flowcharts supported by descriptive narrative.

PROGRAM MANUAL

Table of Contents

1.0 Identification

2.0 Program Description

  2.1 Processing Specification

  2.2 Program Methodology

3.0 Data Specifications

  3.1 File

  3.2 Input

  3.3 Output

4.0 Program Logic

  4.1 Logic Flowchart

  4.2 Tables and Techniques

5.0 Listings

  5.1 Post-assembly Listing

  5.2 Label and Symbol Tables

  5.3 Instruction Listing

  5.4 Switch List

6.0 Program Test Plan

Figure 5.1 Sample Table of Contents—Program Manual

Much has been written about representation of program logic by flow-charts and standards for their presentation. The following simple rules are suggested for the preparation of flowcharts.

1. A macro-flowchart (also known as an outline flowchart) may be prepared (if program size and complexity warrant) to show the basic logical processing steps. If a macro-flowchart is prepared, it should be cross referenced in some manner to the second, "micro" level of flow-charting.

2. The logic of all programs must be shown by micro flowcharts (also known as detailed flowcharts). Coding will in effect take place from the micro-flowchart.

3. Rules may be established for

- size of flowchart paper
- standard symbols to be used
- methods for use of connectors and indicating direction of flow
- methods of presenting information within a symbol

Example rules are given in Appendix B.

4. A cross reference system may be used to relate macro-flowchart to micro-flowchart to coding. Such a system for example could be similar to the one outlined in Appendix B. These, then, would be the areas in which presentation standards for flowcharting could be established. Flowcharts drawn according to the agreed conventions would be included in the sub-section "Logic Flowcharts."

Supporting the diagrammatic representation of logic is a sub-section *Tables and Techniques*. This is generally an optional sub-section: it can be used to describe any special techniques or tables. Tables and techniques which are self-explanatory by reference to the program listing do not require any special description. However, some explana-tory notes may be required for such items as

- complex table structures
- special search techniques
- randomizing formulae
- special access formulae
- core storage layouts for small machines with wiring boards or where buffering techniques are complex

Listings

The coding of the program should be shown by including

- post assembly listing
- label and symbol tables

- machine code instruction listing
- switch list

The listing of the source language program should be a copy of the final assembly listing. The label and symbol tables and machine code instruction listing may be included in the post assembly listing. When they are not so included, separate listings should be produced and incorporated in the Program Manual.

The switch listing should record a list of all program switches under the programmer's control. Notes should be given on the purpose of each switch and the alternate (on/off) settings or conditions.

The coding of a program, as shown in the computer listings, should itself represent a major documentation aid. For example, an assembler or low level language program may be written in accordance with rules which govern program layout and use of labels or symbols. Examples of areas in which rules may be specified are as follows.

1. Layout of introductory comments by use of comment cards showing program and programmer identification, equipment requirements and program options, etc.

2. Layout and content of data defining part of a program, e.g.,

- sequence in which various areas of memory are assigned such as input/output areas, work areas, tables, constants (data and address), messages, headings, halts, and so on
- use of standard identification characters and format for labels. This can include rules of use of first character of label field to show type of field area, e.g.,

    A = accumulator/count field
    D = disk input/output area
    H = halt constant/address
    S = program switch
    K = data constant
    L = table
    M = message
    N = address constant

    Further rules may specify how the remainder of the label is to be made up.
- use of comment cards and comment fields to explain the purpose and use of the field or area

3. Layout of program in terms of blocks, use of block identification comments and block identification character, and listing spacing.

4. Format of source statement (instruction labels). This could include a system which cross references macro- and micro-flowchart to the listing. For example,

first character = B (Branch Point)

second character = block identification character

remainder = numeric character corresponding to the identification sequence numbers on micro-flowchart symbols.

5. Use of comments to describe processing statements. Rules may be specified governing the use of comment cards or the comment field in the processing part of the program. Such rules may include

- abbreviation of comments should be avoided
- comments should be a meaningful description of an operation rather than a simple restatement of an instruction in English language form
- during program testing and alteration, comments as well as instructions should be updated

The actual format and content of comments to certain processes may be standardized as in, for example, the description of entry, processing and exit conditions from a loop.

By the application of such rules, a source program listing of a low or intermediate level language may be constructed so as to form a meaningful document for reference.

Program Test Plan

The preparation of a program test plan is a fundamental technique of program preparation methodology. The basic purpose and use of a test plan is summarized below.

A test plan is essentially a schedule of sequenced operations to test a program. Program testing is perhaps the most inexact science within the programming function; however, it is possible to structure a hierarchy of testing objectives. A suggested breakdown of program test steps is as follows.

1. Rectify clerical or punching errors as indicated by error flags in program listing.

2. For each program block, test using artificial data of simplest cases to test major logic; if the processing reaches end of block compare output to expected result. If correct, test next "logic type." If incorrect or program hangs up, begin major check out by establishing last point that program was functioning correctly and work from there, checking

the contents of key fields, arithmetic accuracy, possibly by use of a trace/diagnostic routine.

3. Continue test using more complex cases and combinations of test cases, to prove each block.

4. Test the overall logic of the program, e.g., interblock communication.

From the above simplified description it can be seen that a good testing technique is a modular technique. Further, testing must not be assumed to be a one-time process. Any but the simplest corrections to a proved program must be followed by a complete testing cycle. Testing is also generally the most time consuming and expensive of the program development tasks. For these reasons, it is important to have a record of the test plan.

The test plan incorporated in the Program Manual should normally comprise

- a summary of method
- list of test cases, sequence of application and expected results
- listing of test data

A major cause of wasted machine time is that program errors are corrected but the test data is not updated. Often, test data is as much in error as the program. Thus, test data, where faulty, should be corrected at the same time as program bugs and documentation are updated. Subsequent testing for program modifications and amendments may thus be made without complete redesign of test data. The other aspect of the test plan is as a control document recording the number of test shots, types of errors and so on.*

This then, is the traditional Program Manual. But as observed at the beginning of this section, it has a number of basic limitations and does not make use of a number of modern techniques.

THE PROGRAM MANUAL—ALTERNATIVE APPROACHES

There are a number of limitations to the arrangement of a Program Manual as described above. There are alternative ways of presenting data other than, for example, by the use of decision tables. Secondly, there are a number of factors in the current methodology of programming which need be considered when determining the type, level and scope of a Program Manual.

* This is covered in *Project Control*, to be published by Brandon/Systems Press, 1969.

The Program Manual as described above would probably be best suited to an installation which has:

- the majority of its programs written in a low level assembly language (such as Autocoder and Easycoder),
- a personnel breakdown in the programming function to program logic designer, coder, and tester,
- little or no elaborate use of application software, and
- a medium to low level of programmers using conventional approaches and techniques

A number of factors which influence the program documentation techniques for different environments are discussed below. These are:

- Logic Representation by Decision Tables
- Impact of High Level Languages
- Impact of Application Packages
- Use of General Purpose Software

As a summary, we may say that the only areas which are not affected by any differences in working environments are Identification, Data Descriptions and Test Plan.

Logic Representation by Decision Tables

Decision tables, previously introduced in the last chapter and described in brief in Appendix C, page 167, can form an effective method of representing detailed program logic. They will usually be backed up by a general narrative description and, for a complex program, a macro-level flowchart.

Decision tables, as is the case with the more conventional flowcharts, can be an integral part of the programming function. That is, they are part of the development process rather than a post-task recording of what has been done.

Decision tables may be used in a number of ways in the programming function. At the lowest level, they may be used only as documentation aids to show complex logical processes. In some cases, they may be used to support flowchart representation and in other cases they may be used as the sole method of logic representation. At the next level of use, the program may be coded directly from and cross referenced to a decision table. Further, a decision table may actualy be set up in memory and be used by the program during processing. At yet another level, decision tables may comprise the source language. The output from a compilation is a high level language object program in a language such as COBOL or FORTAN. An object program thus produced would then be compiled to give a machine code object program. The use of such decision table preprocessors may well obviate the need for detailed manual documentation, since a satisfactory level of automatic documentation may be produced at compilation time.

Use of High Level Languages

The traditional Program Manual as described previously was mainly oriented towards the lower level assembler-type languages. In such a case, it was suggested that reference to program structure and content could be streamlined by using an identification method which directly relates macro-flowchart to micro-flowchart to coding. The use of a high level language would to a large extent make such a system unnecessary and unwieldly. However, to ensure clarity of meaning in the listings a number of simple rules may be laid down. For example, program layout standards may be established for COBOL programs. These could cover such areas as

- rules for the use of an identification character preceding the label to identify it as an accumulator, block, constant, data, etc.
- rules for forming labels (e.g. avoidance of non-standard abbreviations)
- rules for use of comments and paging
- rules for use of margins for lining up source statement entries and for the use of indentations

The required level of flowcharting for a high level language should be at least a macro-level flowchart and, possibly to micro-level flowchart.

For example, a COBOL program which merely produces a number of reports from a file may have a complex "logic structure" but since the program may be a series of similar operations, no micro-flowchart may be required.

Impact of Application Packages

With the wide range of application packages (wide both in terms of scope and quantity) coming onto the market, it is difficult to make generalizations about their impact on program documentation. A prime requirement for an application package is that it be well documented. This is essential, for an inadequately documented package prevents the user from understanding the techniques and methods used. One result of this is that the user is prevented from evaluating its efficiency or effectiveness. In addition, the format and context of the programming and operations documentation may not, however, be written in accordance with the installations standards and therefore require alteration and expansion.

As a basic rule, the level of documentation required for programs comprising an application package should be equivalent to the Program Manual. At least the Identification, Data Description and (probably) the Program Description must be written by the user. Ideally, the logic flowcharts/explanatory narrative/decision tables should be supplied by the developer; the program listings are invariably supplied and the test data is rarely supplied. Depending on the current status of a package, no logic flowcharts may be supplied if the package is at an early state of development. In this case, the user will probably have to undertake the task of preparing flowcharts from the listings. (Alternatively, the flowcharts may not be up-to-date.) If the package is in a more advanced state of development, detailed logic diagrams *may* be available, but, more probably, they will be in outline (with brief narrative) only.

One of the criteria for selecting a particular package, must be the availability and level of documentation supplied.

If the package program documentation is considered adequate, the required Program Manuals may be treated the same way as for the use of general purpose software, as described below.

Use of General Purpose Software

Program documentation should be produced for all programs in a system, including standard utility programs, e.g., sort/merge programs and transcription programs. However, since such software programs are well documented when initially written, the user program documentation can be much abbreviated.

For compatibility, a Program Manual similar in form to the one described can be produced for each utility employed. The manual content would be amended as follows:

Program Methodology—statement of routine name, version number, source, reference to descriptive material, and basic description of parameters (such as sort keys).

Program Logic—detailed list of parameters (e.g., blocking factors, record formats, sort control keys) and parameter card layout and contents; if the software used is a Program Report Generator, the completed specification forms should be included.

Program Coding—listings need be included only for a report generator and similar generator programs.

Similarly, where standard subroutines are incorporated into a program (other than basic input/output subroutines called by an assembler or compiler), these subroutines need not be documented in detail. Standard subroutines used in a program should be referenced in Program Methodology by listing:

- subroutine name
- source/reference
- brief purpose and description
- calling sequence

SOFTWARE DOCUMENTATION

In general, a user written software program should be documented in a complete Program Manual. Considerable detail is needed in all sections of the Manual, but attention should be paid to the Program Description so that the general scope and structure of the program is readily apparent to another programmer. The Program Methodology sub-section should list, in detail, the equipment requirements, the parameters which should be supplied, the acceptance limits for input and the format options of the output.

Large companies may establish a central library with a software index as described in Chapter 9. Consideration must therefore be given to the preparation of a catalogue, giving a brief abstract for each available program. Ideally, the Program Description and the Program Methodology sub-sections should be prepared so that they (complete or in part) serve as the program abstract (see Chapter 9).

SUMMARY

1. The start of the development programming phase is considered to be the provision of authorized Program Specification(s).

2. The end of the development programming phase is the output of proved program(s), fully documented in Program Manual(s).

3. The basic steps in programming are:

- Logic Analysis
- Coding
- Desk Checking
- Test Case Preparation
- Assembly/Compilation and Testing
- Specification of Operating Requirements

- Final Documentation
- Installation

4. The work in the tasks listed above should be documented in a Program Manual. The basic content of a Program Manual is:

- a general description of program functions,
- specification of program logic,
- coding information,
- description of inputs, outputs, files and instructive output messages,
- test plan, and
- program test and operating instructions

5. The establishment of program documentation standards should take into account:

- the level of the language used,
- the use of decision tables,
- the use of general purpose software, and
- the use and selection of application packages

CHAPTER 6

Operations Documentation

In the areas of analytical, system and program documentation discussed in the previous chapter of this part, it was seen that the three documentation classifications corresponded reasonably well with the functional areas of systems design/project management and programming. Operations documentation cuts across the boundaries of these functional areas. Some operations documentation will be prepared by the systems function and some by the programming function. Similarly, some operations documentation must be prepared for the user and some for the data processing operations staff; this is discussed in the next chapter. Thus, it is important to realize that in this chapter we are considering documentation produced by several functional areas. The two basic operations documents are: Program Test Instructions and System Operating Instructions; the latter has a major sub-set: Program Operating Instructions.

PROGRAM TEST INSTRUCTIONS

This document comprises those instructions which are necessary to guide the computer operator in running a program test and are prepared by the programmer. The responsibilities for ensuring that adequate test instructions are prepared should rest with the programming supervisor (chief programmer, team leader, lead programmer, etc.). An additional checkpoint should be considered whereby the senior computer operator may withold or abandon a test shot if the test instructions are ambiguous or incomplete.

In effect, the Program Test Instructions may be prepared with a format and content similar to the Program Operating Instructions discussed later in this chapter. However, it is good programming practice in operational programs to minimize the amount of external communication with the operator. On the other hand, during program testing, additional provision should be made in the test instructions for special procedures, e.g., for programmed breakpoints and even programmer intervention under certain conditions.

SYSTEM OPERATING INSTRUCTIONS

This document comprises a list of processing steps, in the sequence in which they are to be executed, defining, in detail, all the operating requirements. A major subset of this document is the Program Operating Instructions discussed below. Other information which may be included in the System Operating Instructions is:

1. Summary workflow/schedule
2. Data collection and preparation instructions
3. Input control instructions
4. Job assembly instructions
5. Output review and control instructions

At this point in the chapter, a major qualification must be made defining the relationship between the operations documentation and user aids. In some installations functions 2, 3 and 5 may be classed as user functions. That is, the user is given the responsibility for submitting clean data in a form ready for input to a computer. The data processing operations function is simply responsibile for performing the required computer processing and possibly some ancilliary equipment processing. The user is responsible for the subsequent output validation and distribution. However, in another installation the responsibility for these functions may be assumed by data processing operations. In the latter case the user is responsible for providing, in conjunction with the data processing development staff, explicit instructions as to how data is to be handled on receipt from source through to final dispatch. In the former case, the information given for functions 2, 3 and 5 would comprise part of the System Operating Instructions.

The relationship between the contents of the two documents is thus primarily one of functional responsibility between user and data processing operations. For explanatory purposes in this and the next chapter, it is assumed that the user is responsible for submitting source data in accordance with an agreed time and quality schedule. All processing is then performed by data processing operations. The operations documentation therefore conforms to the brief listing of contents as shown on page 103. The required user aid information would include the agreed schedule of times, input quality control information and notes for the interpretation of output reports. Thus, for any other type of working environment the content of the System Operating Instructions and User Aids may be altered or switched according to the division of responsibility. The major requirement is that the information must be available in some formal document and the assignment of responsibilities between operations and the user clearly defined.

Basic Approaches to Organization

The structure of the System Operations Instructions depends on the internal organization structure of operations group. One method of preparing the System Operating Instructions is to prepare one complete specification as shown in the example table of contents on page 103. The material is divided into a logical grouping by functional responsibility within the operations group, prefaced by a summary which shows all the processing steps in sequence. A master copy of the manual may then be kept in the library, a working master by the Operations Manager (or equivalent), and Section 1 plus other relevant section(s) retained by the appropriate operations functions.

Note that this documentation is all job dependent and must be supplemented by general housekeeping documentation such as: tape/disk, library documentation, computer and ancillary equipment usage recording, general quality control requirements, job scheduling and control procedures.

The material presented under the headings shown in Figure 6.1 will be discussed later in this chapter. As with most areas of documentation, there are a multiplicity of different methods for presenting the material, ranging from the use of general narrative within standard headings to the use of preprinted forms. In both cases, the responsibility for ensuring that the System Operating Instructions to the project leader or equivalent. A formal checkpoint should be established for the handover of the operational system and documented instructions to the operations function. The example shown on page 103 is primarily based on the narrative approach. An alternative approach is to use standard preprinted forms and to describe each processing step in sequence. For each process type (e.g., a program run, keypunching a transaction, or an ancillary equipment operation like a tabular listing) there is a standard form to be completed. The forms are bound in the sequence in which they occur, the whole document being again prefaced by an overall workflow summary and schedule. Each operations function holds a complete set of the System Operating Instructions.

Of the two approaches, the latter has been found to work well in most instances. It imposes a strict discipline on the systems analysts and programmers, is easy to use provided the summary section is adequate, and is easy to amend. It is especially useful where the system operation comprises a number of clerical and ancillary operations between computer runs, or where a number of transaction types are to be processed at a different time in the operating cycle. Where most applications comprise a series of more or less consecutive runs, with few intervening clerical or ancillary machine operations, the narrative approach to documentation will probably be adequate. For the purposes of this book, the preprinted form with one form per operation type filed in sequence by operation will be used for explanatory purposes. However, for all but the simplest clerical operations, the printed forms will reflect the physical characteristics of the equipment used. In the following discussion therefore, the minimum headings on the forms will be listed; these must be supplemented where necessary with additional hardware-oriented headings.

The first step in establishing standard System Operating Instructions is to design the required range of forms. A basic range of forms would include

- workflow summary
- general clerical
- data preparation—(i.e., keypunching)
- ancillary machine (by machine category)
- computer operating (by computer type)

A sample Workflow Summary Form is shown in Figure 6.1. Note that the form basically consists of a process flowchart and a process step number column. In the example shown, additional summary information is given for operations control such as volumes and schedule. Each process symbol corresponds to one or more operating instruction forms referenced by the step number. Where the sequence of operations is variable, e.g., the sequence is dependent on the conditions prevailing at the time, alternative sequences may be shown by means of a decision symbol and alternative flow lines.

Each operating instruction form should bear the basic identifying information comprising at least

- system identification
- operation identification (brief title)

Process Step No.	Operation (Process) Flowchart	Specification No.	Volumes	Latest Time To This Operation	Latest Time Out From This Operation
1	Check receipt of batches from all stores	1.1	17 batches of approx. 900 to 1200 documents	10.00 Tuesday	12.00 Tuesday
2	Punch/Verify Issue/Receipts	1.2	17,000 cards	12.00 Tuesday	17.00 Thursday
3	Balance Batches	1.3	N/A	17.15 Thursday	19.00 Thursday
4	Agreement? — N → Error Check to Source — Y	2.0		Variable	
5	Prepare Monthly Parameter Cards	1.4	N/A	08.45 Friday	09.00 Friday
6	Take-on Program 'JM 37'	1.5	17,000 cards 120 forms	09.00 Friday	11.45 Friday

Figure 6.1 Sample Workflow Summary

- this operation step number
- previous operation step number/next operation step number
- date of issue
- originator/authority

Similarly, a number of standard entries may appear beneath the identification block on all forms. These may include

- responsibility for performing the operation
- input: description and source
- output: description and destination
- process: summary of process

A *General Clerical Form* should be used for any manual machine independent operation and thus contains only the above standard identification block and headings. The remainder of the form is "free form" and is completed as required with a detailed specification of the operations to be performed. Entries for various types of operations will be discussed later in this chapter.

The *Keypunch Form* should have provision for recording (or referencing) the following information:

1. Format of Punching Document and Media. This specifies the

- punching code
- an annotated copy of a punching document (if complex), referenced to the appropriate card columns/character positions to be punched
- brief list of card columns/characters stating as content of field alphabetic, numeric, fixed length or variable length and special punching codes (e.g., non-standard field separators and special punching codes in data fields)

2. Special Procedures. This lists any non-standard error correction procedures or special labelling requirements. For example:

- special batch or file labels
- non-standard error repunching procedure for paper tape
- error procedure for obvious mistakes or illegible entries on punching documents
- special requirements for batch control checking

3. Punch Document/Media Destination. This specifies the procedure for disposing of the punching documents and the destination of the punched media.

4. Machine Set-Up. This specifies

- copy of program card/wiring diagram
- switch settings

A pre-printed *Ancillary Equipment Form* should be prepared for each major ancillary machine type. The form should provide for a statement of

- disposition of input/output on machine
- switch settings
- wiring diagrams
- special error/batch checking procedures and a step by step summary of operation, if warranted by complexity of the operation

It is often useful in a large installation running complex applications to have separate *Job Assembly Instructions* prior to the operating instructions for each program. The job assembly instructions list the complete data/program availability requirements for the job to be run. The required material may thus be checked off and assembled in the computer room prior to the program being run. Where it is the responsibility of the job assembly function to prepare parameter cards, the contents, format, and, if necessary, the position of the card in a data file of each parameter card should be given.

The *Computer Operating Instructions* will vary according to the size and type of machine. Note that the operating instructions included in System Operating Instructions are backed up by the relevant program manual (including the detailed data specifications); thus the operating instructions should provide only a concise but complete specification of the procedures to be followed by the computer operator. A general summary of the contents of the computer operating instructions is given below.

A three-sheet approach is recommended, each sheet being identified by the program name/number, with

sheet 1 = summary data and set-up
sheet 2 = running
sheet 3 = take-down

The summary data on sheet 1 should appear below the standard identification block and contain information such as

- brief description of program functions
- summary of peripheral and core storage usage
- priority (for a multiprogramming system)
- estimated running time (average or by volume)

For program set-up, the following information should be given:

1. The exact program name, media and source.
2. The peripheral on which the program is to be loaded (if necessary).
3. For each item of input data

- the name of the input (for operator identification)
- input peripheral type
- actual peripheral (if necessary)

4. For each item of output data

- the name of the output (for operator identification)
- output peripheral type
- actual peripheral (if necessary)
- peripheral preparation instructions, e.g.,
  printer: paper type and size, number of copies, control loop to be used, lining-up instructions
  card/paper tape: card or paper tape type/color, parity checking requirements if variable, visual labelling to be made.

5. Initial switch settings (if any) on console or peripherals.

Items 1 to 4 may be shown on an annotated system flowchart for the program. The additional output preparation instructions in item 4 may be shown by preprinted headings for each peripheral type. Similarly, if the hardware comprises a switch panel console, a diagrammatic representation of the switches may be shown with provision for marking off the settings.

For sheet 2, program running, the action required for the following should be shown

- normal running
- program error
- peripheral failure
- unexpected halts or looping
- restart procedures

The take-down instructions, sheet 3, should specify the visual labelling required on the output and the disposal instructions.

General Clerical Instructions. It is in the area of the above machine oriented instructions that the use of formal preprinted instructions sheets will be most useful. It is a rigid checklist approach for standard presentation ensuring that all the required information will be given in a form for each and quick reference by the operations personnel. However, as discussed at the beginning of this section, a general clerical procedures form should be used for non-machine oriented instructions. These include instructions for input data collection, proving and coding, and for output review, dispatch and control. Below are some general checklists for the contents of these instructions. Again it is necessary to emphasize that some of these instructions will be given as user aids, depending on the arrangement of responsibility.

The input data collection, proving and coding instructions should specify

- methods for evaluating acceptability of data
- methods for establishing control over batches of input
- methods for identifying erroneous input
- procedures for tracing input not received as scheduled
- procedures for handling uncontrolled input

To achieve the above, the instructions may include

- lists of originators of source documents/messages by source and document type
- data reception schedules
- source document specimens
- criteria for valid and invalid data
- user personnel directory for query references
- procedures for coding source documents (if required)
- batching procedure in terms of batch size, batch totalling and "batch receipt register"
- disposition of source documents/messages

The output review and dispatch instructions should specify procedures for

- correct formats and acceptable deviations
- number of report copies
- decollating and binding instructions
- labelling and classification instructions
- authorized distribution
- methods of distribution and special handling procedures

These procedures are essentially concerned with the overall format, completeness and distribution of reports. A more rigorous quality control check is generally required on the content and the appropriate instructions for this may include

- rounding and truncating formulae
- cross-footing controls

- invalid data field conditions
- valid and invalid combinations of data
- tests of reasonability to be applied
- tolerances for accuracy
- meaning of special diagnostic codes and flags
- methods for isolating errors and their causes

SUMMARY

1. Two types of operations documentation are required. There are those instructions which must be given to the user so that he may participate in the running of the system, and there are those instructions required by the data processing operating function.

2. The classification of "user" and "data processing" operations documentation depends on the local division of responsibilities for pre- and post-computer processing.

3. This chapter has assumed that the majority of the processing work (i.e., all operations other than data origination and report interpretation) is the responsibility of the data processing operations function.

4. Data processing operations instructions are defined in a document called Systems Operating Instructions. This is prepared jointly by the systems and programming functions, although responsibility for preparation is usually assigned to a senior member of the systems team.

5. The contents of the Systems Operating Instructions were discussed in terms of a Workflow Summary which indexes or references one set of instructions for each discrete operation.

6. The contents of the instructions for each operation type were discussed.

CHAPTER 7

User and Management Aids

User and management aids are the two areas of development documentation that are perhaps the most nebulous in scope and content. Therefore, before presenting some suggested documents, the purposes of user and management documentation should be defined.

User aids comprise that documentation which presents information to enable the user to understand and approve his system, and later to participate in the running of the system. The aspect of user involvement is often overlooked during the systems development work. Often, the user may not actively participate in the systems development because of a past experience of poor relations with data processing or because the failure of data processing personnel to present information in non-technical form suggests a "closed-mind" attitude. More likely, the user may accept and participate passively in the systems development work and in the subsequent system operation. This passive user involvement is perhaps most critical in the area of systems maintenance and improvement. When a system is implemented, data processing staff participation is reduced and the user is forced to accept responsibilities for some parts of its day-to-day operation. When major flaws are uncovered in the operation of the system and the user has not actively participated during the development process, lack of user involvement may result in

- the user instituting his own remedies to problems, thus possibly negating certain functions of the system and countering proposed aims and benefits;
- the user claiming that the whole system is defective rather than specific parts of the system; and

- the user placing complete reliance on data processing for controlling the operation of the system.

Thus, user involvement is of primary importance and user aids are therefore essential aspects of development documentation.

Management aids comprise information to enable senior management to assess the applicability of a system to their needs, assess the benefits of the system, and appreciate the necessary time scale and resources for implementation.

Thus, the distinction between user and management aids is derived from the organizational structure or responsibility assignment within a company. Their common similarity is that they are for non-data processing personnel; their differences are that user aids are primarily concerned with the operation of the system, while management aids comprise summarizations of system function and resource requirements.

Suggested areas for use of user and management aids are in

- Management Summaries
- Reference Manuals
- User Data Processing System Instructions
- User Input Preparation Instructions

MANAGEMENT SUMMARIES

The Management Summaries comprise that part of the System Specifications corresponding to Management Summary described in Chapter 4, page 37. The Management Summary serves two purposes. First, it informs management about current developments within their own area of responsibility. Second, by establishing a management distribution list, the collected Management Summaries may act as a "catalogue" of applications and systems. As described in Chapter 4, these instruction abstracts describe the capabilities and limitations of a system to allow management to evaluate the applicability of a system to a requirement.

REFERENCE MANUALS

The term Reference Manual is used here to cover those documents produced for the user as required. Provision should be made for assigning the responsibility for assessing the need for a Reference Manual to the appropriate project management. Examples of Reference Manuals are given below.

User Guides to Data Processing Services

These Manuals cannot truly be classed as development documentation. They are intended to improve liaison between users and data processing personnel by defining the data processing services which are and are not available and the procedures for requesting reports and systems. These manuals may be backed up by more specific manuals relating to one system. For example, in a large system with a complete and complex data base, a *Guide to Report Requests* may be produced. This manual describes the current reports available and the data content of the files, what may and may not be requested, and the forms to be completed for the request.

Coding Manuals

These manuals describe the structure of, and list in quick reference form, the codes to be used when completing input forms or transaction documents.

Conversion Instructions

System conversion from a manual system to a computer system can represent a major task. These manuals provide a step-by-step guide to conversion. They may therefore act as supplements to Coding Manuals or Training Manuals (see below).

Training Manuals

These manuals are prepared as required to instruct users in the system. Note that they are not the same as specific operating instructions; rather than a concise list of "who does what and when," training manuals explain the overall system and the background to the various aspects of user participation.

The actual contents of the various Reference Manuals will vary widely by type and function. As a general rule, however, as much as possible of the existing system documentation should be used in the preparation of Reference Manuals. The following are some general rules for the preparation of Reference Manuals.

(1) Each manual should comprise a standard introductory section stating

- the name of manual
- its purpose and aims
- its intended readership
- the prerequisites for use

- the authority for preparation
- its organization
- how it should be used and updated

(2) The manual should be written in simple, non-technical language, directed at the level of the particular audience for which it is intended.

(3) Illustrations should be used as necessary, e.g., to show how a form is filled out, how equipment is operated, and the flow of work. When forms are illustrated, they should contain representative sample entries; instructions for completing the form should be keyed to these sample entries.

(4) If it appears that there will be a large number of Reference Manuals produced, standard house rules should be prepared covering general methods of presentation, e.g.,

- basic manual level (e.g., to section, chapter and subject level)
- page numbering system
- Illustrations numbering system
- standard paragraph numbering system
- standard amendment handling and distribution

USER OPERATING INSTRUCTIONS

These are prepared to instruct the user in the procedures for input data preparation and for control of output reports. As discussed in Chapter 6, there will always be a requirement for User Operating Instructions. At the simplest level, these instructions specify the procedures for such operations as completing source documents, the time-table for submission of data, brief descriptions of the content of a printed report (e.g., meaning of error flags).

If the user has a direct responsibility for detailed proving of input etc., the relevant parts of the System Operating Instructions will be the user reference. The complexity of the system may demand additional operating instructions. For example, if the user has access to remote terminals, detailed instructions will be required on their operation and use. Similarly, an off-line data transmission system will require special instructions for call-up and closing messages, batching procedure, transmission times and so on.

SUMMARY

1. User aids comprise those documents submitted to the user so that he may participate in the design and running of a system.

2. User participation is vital to ensure that

- the user's system is workable and represents what he, the user, wants;
- the user is able to submit the correct input at the right time, and is capable of interpreting the output; and
- the user is able to "sustain" the system when data processing development support is reduced when the system is operational.

3. Management aids, in the form of Management Summaries from the System Specification, keep management up-to-date with developments both within and outside their areas of responsibilities.

4. The production of Reference Manuals should be considered as and when required. Example reference manuals quoted were:

- User Guides to Data Processing Services
- Coding Manuals
- Conversion Instructions
- Training Manuals

General rules for the production of Reference Manuals were discussed.

CHAPTER 8

Development Documentation and Project Control

As discussed in Chapter 2, this book is concerned with development documentation, rather than with control documentation (i.e., that documentation produced solely for project control purposes). It was mentioned, however, that standardized development documentation can be used as an aid in project control. This is achieved by establishing formal checkpoints during a development project and by monitoring progress and quality of work at these points by an appraisal of documentation. This chapter discusses the establishment of formal checkpoints with the use of development documentation.

PROJECT PHASES AND TASKS

A data processing project can be segmented into a number of distinct phases, which in turn may be further sub-divided into tasks. Generally any project may be considered as comprising three basic phases: Project Initiation, Project Fulfillment and Project Conclusion. A complete list of tasks within these phases is shown in Figure 8.1. The segmentation of a project as shown in the figure provides management with a capability of monitoring smaller units of activity.

The conclusion of each phase or task may be considered as a project checkpoint. A project checkpoint is therefore established at each point in a project where there is a "turnover" of work from one task to another. For example, the turnover of a Systems Specification to the programming function would require a checkpoint, as would the turnover of programs with associated documentation to the operating function.

117

PROJECT CONTROL POINTS

Project Initiation

     1.   Project Selection
     2.   Project Authorization
     3.   Project Planning
     4.   Personnel Assignment
     5.   Estimating
     6.   Scheduling
     7.   Budgeting

Project Fulfillment

     8.   System Study—1st Phase
     9.   System Study—Completion
     10.   System Analysis Completion
     11.   System Design—Data Base Specification
     12.   System Design Completion
     13.   Programming—Coding Completion
     14.   Programming—Third Machine Test
     15.   Programming—75% of Program Test Budget
     16.   System Test Plan Completion
     17.   System Test—Intermediate Review
     18.   System Test Completion
     19.   Volume Test Plan Completion

Project Conclusion

     20.   Pre-Conversion Preparation Completion
     21.   Post-Implementation Audit

Figure 8.1   Typical project control points

Specific documentation requirements, as well as other requirements, can be defined as marking the completion of a task. The purpose of a checkpoint at the completion of each task is to verify that the work performed so far has been completed satisfactorily and according to established standards. Work does not progress onto the next task unless the work output from the previous task, as reflected in the documentation, is approved in terms of quality (workability and accuracy), completeness and legibility.

Of course, the output from many tasks is a defined product which must also be reviewed, e.g., the review of a program in terms of the quality of its output, running speed and ease of operation. However, in this Chapter, we are primarily concerned with the documentation aspect of project checkpoints. Further, the actual grouping of tasks for any one project and the review criteria at any one checkpoint will depend on the characteristics of a project. This is discussed in Chapter 10 when the considerations for establishing documentation standards for a particular environment are reviewed.

DOCUMENTATION CHECKPOINTS

The development documentation required at each task is discussed below. This documentation is based on the levels and types of documentation as described in Part Two.

Phase 1—Project Initiation

Task 1—Project Selection. Project Selection requires that the project objectives be clearly stated and the project is properly defined and its scope established. The User Request must be completed.

Task 2—Project Authorization. When the user and data processing are ready to proceed, the project objectives are reviewed and accepted. The System Proposal must be completed.

Task 3—Planning. The Project Plan includes a detailed task outline and an analysis of required skills. The Analytical Report and Design Requirements Statements are prepared.

Task 4—Personnel Assignment. The personnel required for the project are assigned in this phase. No new development documentation is prepared.

Task 5—Time Estimating. Analytical documentation and list of project tasks are reviewed in detail; standards are applied for the estimation of time required to complete the project. No new development documentation is prepared.

Task 6—Scheduling. Task estimates are reviewed to develop a total project schedule. No new development documentation is prepared.

Task 7—Budgeting. Tasks and time are listed; standard rates are applied to develop a complete picture of project costs. No new development documentation is prepared.

Phase 2—Project Fulfillment

Task 1—First Stage of Systems Study. The user's initial reaction to the Project Plan is elicited and possible problem areas reviewed. No new development documentation is prepared.

Task 2—Systems Study Completion. The proposed system is reviewed with the user; exceptions and expansions in the scope of the project are identified. All analytical documentation (User Request, Analytical Report, Design Requirements Statement) is reviewed and approved, and the System Summary is prepared.

Task 3—System Analysis Completion. Design alternatives and systems requirements are reviewed and design estimates made. Documentation prepared to date is reviewed and accepted. The System Specification (file, transaction, output, and processing and system test plan) is prepared.

Task 4—Data Base Design Completion. Specifications for files, transactions, outputs and related reports are reviewed, checked against the System Summary, and discussed with and approved by the user.

Task 5—System Design. All System Specifications are reviewed and additional Program Specifications are prepared, if necessary. Specifications for files, input/outputs, reports, controls, processing requirements are prepared and reviewed. Readiness for programming to begin is ascertained.

Task 6—Coding. Logic flow specifications and the program test plan are prepared. Coding is reviewed to insure that it is faithful to the logic design. The program test plan, test data, and instructive output specifications are prepared and reviewed.

Task 7—First Stage of Program Testing. A review of the status of a program is made after the third test. At this point the Programming Specification is reviewed and checked against the initial output. No new development documentation is prepared.

Task 8—Final Stage of Program Testing. The Program Test Plan is checked to ensure that it has been followed. Program test results are also checked against the Program Specification to determine whether results are satisfactory.

Task 9—System Test Plan Completion. Upon completion of program testing, the System Test Plan is reviewed. At the same time, preliminary operating instructions are reviewed and the completion of program testing validated.

Task 10—Interim Stage of Systems Testing. The number of program changes required, running time, program interface, errors, and test results are reveiwed and checked against the Systems Test Plan to determine whether results are satisfactory.

Task 11—System Test Completion. The results of the systems test are checked against the Systems Specification. Changes already made and documentation changes required are reviewed, and user acceptance obtained.

Task 12—Volume Test Plan. All user aids (data input, output, collection, preparation and control instructions), and data processing (system and program) operating instructions are reviewed prior to scheduling a volume test.

Phase 3—Project Conclusion

Task 1—Preconversion Check. Results of the volume test are reviewed to determine adequacy of documentation and readiness for conversion.

Task 2—Post-Implementation Audit. The anticipated system benefits are compared with actual benefits to determine if the system has fulfilled requirements. Needed improvements are identified and documentation changed accordingly.

SUMMARY

1. Standardized documentation, in conjunction with an established system of checkpoints, is a major aid to effective project control.

2. A development project may be divided into three major phases

- Project Initiation
- Project Fulfillment
- Project Conclusion

which may be further sub-divided into a number of tasks as shown in Figure 8.1 on page 118.

3. At the completion of each task a review is made of any documentation prepared during that task.

4. The review of documentation against the prescribed standards should cover

- Workability
- Accuracy

- Legibility
- Completeness

5. Work does not proceed to the subsequent tasks until the review described in item 4 above is satisfactory.

6. Suggested tasks and checkpoints have been discussed in pages 119 to 121.

CHAPTER 9

The Documentation Library and Documentation Maintenance

The term "documentation library" as used in this chapter, relates to a centralized function responsible for the control, retention, storage and distribution of master documentation files. The exact functions and responsibilities of a documentation library will depend on the particular characteristics and requirements of any one company. Some general aspects of the contents and organization of a library are given below.

DOCUMENTATION LIBRARY—ORGANIZATION AND RESPONSIBILITIES

The position of the documentation library within an organization will depend on local conditions. However, in any company but the smallest with little data processing activity, the documentation library must be recognized as a specific independent function. The resources expended on the library will depend on many factors such as

- scope of data processing activities,
- frequency of reference to contents,
- whether data processing functions are centralized or decentralized,
- internal structure of the data processing department, and
- project types.

Depending on the degree of sophistication required of the library, it may have responsibilities for some or all of the following:

1. Review of development documentation to ensure adherence to standards and appropriate authorization of exceptions.
2. Registration and storage of acceptable documentation.
3. Revisions handling.
4. Notification and distribution to interested parties.

At the lowest level of usage, the documentation library may be simply existing for the control, storage, retention and distribution of master development documents, with a part-time librarian. In this case the library would probably contain all final systems development documentation. However, a documentation library may also serve as a control function related to the programming or operations facilities. Thus, it may also act as a control point for software information handling. For example, in a company with a large or decentralized programming capability, summary specifications of all programs produced are filed with the documentation library. In the library the specifications are indexed (say by application, type of program and originator) and copies circulated to programming personnel.

Similarly, the documentation library may be linked to the operations function. In a large installation where many different applications are run, the availability of a program or suite of programs to run may be indicated by the presence or absence of the operations documentation, or a clarification code filed against the operations documentation. The documentation library may also be used to file and update master copies of manufacturer's literature. In some cases, updating software literature for languages and utilities can represent a major task. The library, while maintaining a master set, can also be given the responsibility for distributing manufacturer's material to local working copies. This has the added advantage of having one reception point for all manufacturer's literature.

Thus, as can be seen from the above discussion, the documentation library should initially not only be considered as serving a storage function; it may be used as a central point of control with any other data processing function.

Contents and Procedures

The basic classifications for documentation are

- systems
- program
- operations
- users

Each of the above documentation elements may be grouped into a folder identified by a project or task number. Within each folder may be

- a file log and checklist
- revision notices

- cross reference index or indexes
- distribution list
- development documentation

Note that this information must be included for all projects, even if the project has been suspended, thus forming a master documentation file. This file is up-to-date and complete even though various functional groups may maintain duplicate files pertinent to their own needs. A brief description of the folder content listed above is given below.

The file log records the revisions made and the status of the project, e.g., operational under revision, suspended or obsolete, etc. A checklist is a useful method of ensuring the completion of the documentation in the folder. For each folder type, a standard list of contents should be shown (with space for listing optional additions). Against this list should be space for recording that an item is included, or referencing its location if it has been omitted; examples are shown in Figure 9.1(a)-(d). Revision notices should contain

- project identification and date of revision
- revision originator authorization
- brief summary and scope of revision
- list of attachments detailing the revision

A suggested method of processing revisions is as follows. The librarian should log the appropriate section of a file as soon as it is known that there is a revision in hand. Formal notice of the revision, with appropriate authorization, should be sent to the library where the change is entered into the file log and the required amendments made to the documentation. The cross reference index is then inspected to determine if all appropriate secondary appearances of the information have been covered by the distribution list. The revision is then circulated as per the distribution list.

The cross-reference index(es) lists all folders or files in which a document is duplicated, thus giving an easy means of keeping track of documentation for maintenance purposes.

The actual development documentation should have been prepared in accordance with the laid-down standards. The documents are filed in numerical sequence within the folder.

Within the library, therefore, each documentation element of a project is represented by a folder containing complete information. A subject-reference index may be maintained to permit the rapid location of the individual folders. Note that, in certain instances, information may

SYSTEM FOLDER
DOCUMENT CHECKLIST

Project/Task Number _____ Date _____

Prepared by _____ Approved by _____

Document Name	Included	Document Used as Replacement	Associated Reference Material	Source
SYSTEM NAME				
1. Project/Task Statement (User Request)				
2. Systems Proposal				
3. Analytical Report (name) Attachments: (name & number)				
4. Design Requirements Statement				
5. System Summary				
6. File Specifications: (file name & nos.)				
7. Transaction Specs.				
8. Output Specs.				
9. Segment Processing Specs: (Segment names & nos.)				
10. System Test Plan				

Figure 9.1 (a) System Folder Document Checklist

PROGRAM FOLDER
DOCUMENT CHECKLIST

Project/Task Number _____   Date _____

Prepared by _____ Approved by _____

PROGRAM NAME   PROGRAM NUMBER

Document Name	Included	Document Used as Replacement	Associated Document Reference	Source
11. Programming Specification				
12. Transaction Specification				
13. Instructive Output Specification				
14. Internal Flow Specification				
15. Programming Parameters				
16. Program Test Plan				

Figure 9.1 (b) Program Folder Document Checklist

OPERATIONS FOLDER
DOCUMENT CHECKLIST

Page   of

Project/Task Number_____ Date _____

Prepared by_____   Approved by _____

SYSTEM NAME

Document Name	Included	Document Used as Replacement	Associated Document Reference	Source
17. Program Test Instructions				
18. System Setup Instructions				
19. System/Program Operating Instructions				
20. Input Collection and Preparation Instructions				
21. Input Control Instructions				
22. Output Review and Distribution Instructions				
23. Output Control Instructions				

Figure 9.1 (c) Operations Folder Document Checklist

FILE HISTORY FORM

REVISION PAGE

Date	Section	Chapter	Page	Reviser	Approval Initials	Purpose	Description

Figure 9.1(d)   File History Form — Revision Page

appear in more than one folder; repetition of the information, rather than the use of cross-references, allows each folder to be used separately and facilitates the maintenance and control of distribution. The documentation relating to general-purpose programs or files used by more than one program should be stored in the originating project/task file. However, it is often useful for an additional copy of this documentation to be filed separately under a general-purpose documentation category.

Within this general framework for the library, specific procedures must be specified for

- method of review to ensure that documentation is prepared in accordance with the standards
- registering (indexing and storing) acceptable documentation
- recording and distribution of revised information and project status
- record of loans/returns from the library

DOCUMENTATION MAINTENANCE

The key to the successful use of documentation is that it must be maintained—it must be current and represent the exact requirements and methodology of a system. Thus, any standardization of documentation must specify the authority, control and techniques for documentation maintenance.

Authority and Control

The placement of authority for ensuring that systems and operating changes are correctly documented depends on the project development "team" structure. However, in most instances, overall responsibilities for documentation are maintained by the technical project personnel. The actual mechanics of distributing and recording amendments are the responsibilities of a documentation library as described previously in this chapter.

Thus, for a major systems change, a suggested procedure for documentation updating is as follows:

1. Project leader obtains master copy of systems documentation library.
2. Project leader reviews master documentation and notes areas (sections) where revision is necessary.
3. Project personnel process the required changes and draft documentation revision(s).

4. Project leader reviews work, documentation and obtains revision authority from appropriate parties.

5. Submit revision notice(s), plus attachments(s) to library.

6. Documentation library processes revisions.

Techniques

The actual techniques for revising the documentation will depend on the nature of the changes and the structure of the documentation. Within the documentation standards, explicit rules must be given for amendments. Some general considerations are given below. Documentation amendment procedures should make provision for the following types of changes.

1. Changes which can be made directly on existing documentation without making it illegible or unintelligible.

2. Additions which amplify, clarify or augment existing documentation without making obsolete the present contents.

3. Changes which are a whole or partial replacement of existing documentation.

SUMMARY

1. The basic responsibilities of the documentation library are the control, retention, storage and distribution of master documentation files.

2. The position of the documentation library in the organizational structure is dependent on conditions. However, for all but the small data processing installations, consideration should be given to establishing the documentation library as a specific independent function.

3. The conditions which influence the establishment of a documentation library have been discussed, and additional functions of the library in the programming and operations areas were suggested.

4. The contents of the library were discussed in terms of a "folder" comprising documentation housekeeping information and the actual development documentation itself. Critical procedures for processing these folders in the library were outlined.

5. Documentation maintenance is a major area in which rigid standards should be specified *and enforced.*

6. The documentation library can be used to control documentation maintenance distributions. Procedures should be established for maintenance techniques and amendment originator/library/recipient communication.

CHAPTER 10

Development of Documentation Standards

Thus far in this book, we have reviewed the requirements for a standard system of documentation, identified the main types of documents and described a basic level of document content. This chapter discusses the problems facing a company which has decided to prepare definitive documentation standards.

As discussed in Chapter 2, there is no one universal documentation system which is valid for all environments. How then can a company produce its own individual documentation standards? If we accept that computer aided information processing has been with us for a quarter of a century, there is obviously no basis for any company starting at "ground zero." The experience gained in the industry in only the last five years should be a sufficient basis for embarking on a documentation standards program without repeating the same groundwork covered previously many hundreds of times. Thus, the development of documentation standards should to a large extent be a process of *adaptation* rather than *origination*. The information presented in Part II of this book should provide an adequate technical starting point for the production of documentation standards for a particular company.

The development of company documentation standards may be only a subsidiary project to the production of a comprehensive set of company data processing standards. Such standards would include methodology for all data processing tasks, and possibly performance standards for personnel and equipment. The requirements for developing company methods and performance standards are described in *Management Standards for Data Processing* by Dick H. Brandon (Van Nostrand, Princeton, N.J., 1963). This chapter considers only the development of documentation standards rather than complete company data processing standards. But, as discussed previously, this exercise in itself can lead to a certain amount of standardization in methodology, since the end product of a task has been clearly defined.

Irrespective of the scope of the standards program, to achieve any worthwhile output will require *management backing;* a belief by management that standards *are* necessary, that the expending of resources *will* lead to a product which will enhance the company's data processing effort. Besides the commitment of resources to a "non-productive" function, management must recognize that their backing is essential for standards enforcement. They must also be prepared to accept that time scales for some projects will be extended (compared to similar work performed previously) to compensate for the learning period of the new standards. Similarly, time scales may be extended to make allowances for more rigid documentation requirements; e.g., the current average of 5% of project time spent on documentation may be increased to 20% after the standards are implemented.

Thus, bearing in mind this major emphasis on the importance of management backing, we may now consider the outputs from and tasks in, a documentation standards development program.

The output of the standards development program should be

- a Manual of Documentation Standards
- a maintenance and support program
- a training and implementation scheme

The tasks which must be performed to achieve the above output may be grouped into three phases

- Preparatory tasks
- Development tasks
- Post-implementation tasks—audit, maintenance and support

These tasks are discussed in detail below.

PREPARATORY TASKS

A documentation standards development project may be compared with a systems development project. It must be subject to the same controls, planning and resource allocation. Further, a standards development project will require analysis of the current environment, projections of future requirements, design of a product, development of maintenance functions, audit of finished product and so on. Thus, the preparatory tasks in a standards development project may be likened to the project initiation phase in a systems development project.

The three major preparatory tasks are

- Establish organization of the project and allocation of resources
- Define scope of standards program
- Define organization of the Manual

and are discussed below.

Project Organization and Resource Allocation

The key to a successful standards project is usually the initial planning. The planning serves three aims

- to provide a master plan for project development,
- to assure precise understanding of task assignments and respon- sibilities,
- to establish a control system for the project to monitor quality and progress.

The ways and means by which these three aims are met depends, of course, on the size, organization and attitude of a particular company. However, some methods which have been found by experience to work well are discussed below.

Of equal weight to the prerequisite of management backing is the complementary requirement that the personnel actively concerned with the project consider it as a first or second priority task. Without man- agement backing, the "working priority" of the standards project may be relegated to a fifth- or sixth-priority rating behind all productive project work. For large companies, an independent function of "Stand- ards Development" may be created. This would comprise a staff work- ing full time on standards co-ordination and development. Any other alternative approach to the separate standards function will lead to problems. A common case is the assignment of the various areas for standardization to the relevant technical specialists. Without a strong coordination function for consolidation of the various outputs, the standards manual degenerates into a collection of informal papers. These may be written in different styles, in various levels of detail, in a multitude of formats and so on.

A simple approach to developing standards is the Review Committee/ Working Committee approach. The Review Committee functions as the policy decision making body; it also serves as review function for final output. For continuity therefore, it should comprise the same permanent members. The composition of the committee will depend on the local company structure. For example, in a company with a number of completely decentralized data processing functions, the Review Committee would comprise all divisional data processing managers. Thus, the first task is to organize the Review Committee; that is, define its function and composition.

The Working Committee is responsible for the actual preparation of draft material. Since, as we shall see later, the manual will be divided into sections, each section dealing with different functional areas (programming, systems, operating, etc.), the composition of the Working Committee will be flexible. Thus, the second task is the organization of a Working Committee. Initially, the general items of reference must be established and its method of working defined. As the scope and contents of the standards manual are agreed, the assignment of responsibilities for the Working Committee is made as members are seconded to the committee.

Having formulated the "charts," liaison procedures between the committees and their members must be defined including procedures for scheduling meetings, recording and distributing results, and review methods. After the standards manual has been released, the Review Committee should function in the auditing of the standards for effectiveness and in the review of new or revised material.

At this stage in the project there will probably be at least a rough draft of the table of contents of the standards manual. An initial arrangement can therefore be made for the allocation of personnel in the "Standards Development Group" (if applicable) required to develop each section in the manual.

Project Scope

The first act of the Review Committee is to define the scope of the standards development program, if this has not been specified precisely by higher management.

That is to

- define the levels and type of material to be included in the standards program
- identify overlapping between current operating procedures and proposed standards

Of major importance is the definition of the limits of the standards project: is the project to cover methodology standards, performance standards and documentation standards? Similarly, what general approach is to be used in a decentralized company in the area of "local" standards? An example of the latter is where one company comprises a number of decentralized data processing development functions, each function having a different project mix and working environment. The standards manual may specify mandatory standards for all "divisions" but a procedure would probably be necessary for the inclusion of local standards peculiar to each division.

It should now be possible to define a firm outline table of contents for the manual and to assign the responsibility and authority for the development of each section in the manual.

Finally, the relationship between the standards project and other procedures and policies must be clearly established and a method of coordination agreed. Most companies, for example, issue management directions on policy. These "company instructions" may or may not have precedence over the standards manual; after the issue of the standards manual all statements of data processing organization and policy may be issued as an amendment to the manual, rather than by the issue of a company instruction.

Organization of the Manual

Having defined the general scope of the manual, the actual content may now be planned in terms of the logical order of the content and the physical format of the manual. As an indication of the layout of a documentation standards manual, a sample table of contents is given in Figure 10.1. The actual sequence of the material will, of course, depend on the particular environment of one company. (More will be said about content later in this chapter.)

In addition to defining the logical order of content, the physical format of the manual should be determined in terms of

- structure of manual
- indexing and page numbering system
- positioning and referencing of illustrations
- page layout and identification block
- distribution requirements and procedures
- methods of reproduction

A commonly used structure requires a breakdown to section, chapter and subject. This gives a referencing system of S.C.s, where S = section number, C = chapter number, and s = subject number. For ease of amendment and identification, pages should be numbered within each subject.

DATA PROCESSING STANDARDS

AND PROCEDURES MANUAL

Table of Contents

Documentation Section

10.0 Documentation Standards

10.1 Documentation Requirements
10.1.1 Documentation Library
10.1.2 Project/task document file
10.1.3 Procedures and responsibilities
10.1.4 Documentation conventions

10.2 Systems Analysis and Design Documentation
10.2.1 Preliminary studies and proposals
10.2.2 General system description
10.2.3 Input/Output description
10.2.4 Detailed system description
10.2.5 System testing

10.3 Programming Documentation
10.3.1 General program description
10.3.2 Input/output description
10.3.3 Detailed program description
10.3.4 Program testing

10.4 Operations Documentation
10.4.1 Test operations
10.4.2 Job operation
10.4.3 Input management
10.4.4 Output management

10.5 Reference Documentation
10.5.1 User's Guide
10.5.2 Technical Guide

Figure 10.1 Sample Table of Contents for Documentation
from a DP Standards Manual

Similarly, illustrations (referred to as Exhibits or Attachments) should be numbered within subjects. Thus, the basic unit of work is the subject.

Within each subject, the treatment given to the material will depend on the working environment. One approach is to make the presentation of material below subject level informal. Beyond defining that an ordered system of indentation of headings is to be used to break up the text and that paragraphs giving individual rules are to be numbered, no other format standards may be imposed.

On the other hand, in a large or complex manual rules may be defined for the presentation of material. For example, each subject may begin with two standard headings: Purpose (of the subject) and References (to related subjects). The remainder of the subject is developed, within a prescribed paragraph layout and numbering system, as the material dictates. An example of format and layout rules for a presentation which is generally applicable is given below.

Example Rules

1. The manual will be divided into

   - sections
   - chapters
   - subjects

2. The numbering system to be used is S.C.s, where S = section, C = chapter and s = subject. Pages will be numbered within subjects and referenced as S.C.s-p, where p is the page number.

3. The first page of each subject will contain an identification block thus

SECTION	
CHAPTER	
SUBJECT	Date of Issue:

4. Continuation pages must have the page numbers only in the form S.C.s-p, in the upper right hand corner of the page.

5. Illustrations must be numbered within subject in the form S.C.s-e and referred to in the text as Exhibits. All exhibits should be grouped in sequence at the end of a subject.

6. Exhibits should be identified by the caption
            ["Subject S.C.s Exhibit e. page P."]
on the bottom right-hand corner of the page.

7. References to an exhibit contained in the same subject should by

"see Exhibit e" or "as shown in Exhibit e" etc. References to an exhibit in another subject should be by "see Exhibit S.C.s-e" or "as shown in Exhibit S.C.s-e", etc.

8. Immediately beneath the identification block on the first page of a subject should be a brief summary of contents as shown in the example in Figure 10.2.

9. Each subject will be broken down into a number of paragraphs according to logical content. Each paragraph will be identified by a heading typed in capitals and underlined, and a paragraph number (see Figure 10.2).

10. The first two paragraphs in each subject will be "1. PURPOSE" and "2. REFERENCES." Paragraph 1 is a brief, one or two sentence, description of the content of the subject. Paragraph 2 will contain applicable references to other subjects or other material (e.g., company instructions or programmer's reference manuals).

11. If a further breakdown is required within a paragraph, such as in a list of items, each item must be identified by a lower case alphabetic character.

12. The writing style will depend on the type of material presented. Specific mandatory standards must be written in an authoritarian style, breaking up the material into a list of precise statements as described in 11 above. Where general guidelines are given, narrative text presented in an instructional style may be used.

In addition to the above rules, general notes may be provided as the job progresses on such subjects as

- standard spelling where alternatives are available
- use of capital letters for job titles and forms, etc.
- use of imperative and conditional expressions, and standard tenses (e.g., rules for use of "must", "should" and "will")

By this stage, therefore, the content, scope and layout of the manual will have been determined. Work may thus begin on the development tasks.

DEVELOPMENT TASKS

Within the policy, scope, contents and format definition previously agreed, development work may now commence in detail. The standards development process may be subdivided into twelve tasks as summarized in Figure 10.3. The first four tasks may be grouped together for explanatory purposes as "initial development tasks". Because the exact allocation of these tasks and the work involved is so depend-

FORMAT OF STANDARDS MANUAL

SECTION
    Documentation Standards

	section	chapter	subject	page
	1	4	1	

CHAPTER
    Documentation Requirements

SUBJECT
    Documentation Conventions

Paragraph

Purpose	1
References	2
Identification Cover Page	3
Table of Contents	4
Narrative Format	5
Flowcharting Format	6
Table and Exhibit Formats	7
Glossaries	8

1. PURPOSE: This subject defines the rules governing format for the routinely used elements of documentation described in other subjects in this Section of the Manual.

2. REFERENCES:

3. IDENTIFICATION COVER PAGE: This page serves as the title page for each element of documentation, describing the document and specifying the desired coordination, review and approval cycle.

Figure 10.2 Sample layout of Standards Manual

STANDARDS DEVELOPMENT TASKS

Task

I.	Develop Schedule
II.	Define Policies and Procedures
III.	Select Subject Sequence
VI.	Cross Reference Index
V.	Research
VI.	Subject Definition
VII.	Review with Working Committee
VIII.	First Draft Preparation
IX.	Steering Committee Coordination
X.	Final Draft Preparation
XI.	Implementation Definition
XII.	Distribution

Figure 10.3 Standards development tasks

ent on the local environment, they are summarized briefly in list form in Figure 10.4.

We may now review the work involved in developing the actual documentation standards.

The research task is necessary to

- provide the groundwork for development of each standard,
- determine the formal and informal practices now in effect,
- gather data for comparison of the various approaches or possible solutions, and
- establish priority of needs and probability for successful implementation.

In Chapter 3, a brief examination was made of the major factors influencing the type, level of content, and distribution of documentation in any working environment. It was shown that the documentation system employed would vary not only from company to company, but also from project to project within any one company. This is illustrated by the chart shown in Figure 10.5. This chart shows for each project type and by frequency of use, the relative importance of each of the control elements, i.e., quality, time and resources, where "X" indicates most important. A further breakdown by project control points is shown in Figure 10.6. As can be seen from these examples, it is of primary importance to establish documentation standards for all types of projects. It is, of course, impracticable and undesirable to establish one mandatory level for documentation since the chosen level would either be inadequate for a "long term development project" and too complex for a "maintenance rescue project."
One method of catering to this varied project mix is to set standards for the "long term development project" and qualify the requirements for documentation for each other project type.

Thus, having established the project types to be covered in the manual, detailed "data gathering" and research can take place. Principally, research should include the following areas:

- Review of present methods for achieving desired results
- Establish the needs and criteria that the standard must satisfy
- Investigate the various methods and procedures that can fill the needs
- Review any informal standard or method that is being used currently

- Define accountable exceptions to the standard that must be considered
- Document all available information

Based on this research, a definition of the method of presentation and content of each subject may be made in a working level document.

This document can then be presented to the Working Committee. The working document should present

- Logical flow for subject presentation
- The standard(s) to be incorporated
- The scope or technical range of the standard
- The relationship to external policies and procedures that are affected
- Enforcement policy and methods (including documentation control points)

Working Committee Review and Draft Preparation

The Working Committee reviews the working document and validates the accuracy and viability of each of the proposed standards. The output is thus a finalized working document for standards development from which a draft will be prepared for submission to the Review Committee. In the review, special attention should be paid to

- weakness or omissions in the prepared standards
- exceptions because of special conditions
- accuracy of technical data to be included in the final standard

Acting on the comments and discussions in the Working Committee a first draft is prepared for the Review Committee. Ideally, many of the technical points should have been validated or rejected by the Working Committee. Thus, the Review Committee should function primarily as a final quality control check, reviewing policy aspects of the prepared standards and ensuring management support for the implementation of the standards.

To enable a comprehensive review to be made, the draft should be prepared by block of subjects, forming at least one self-contained unit of information. All reference material must be prepared, including special forms and/or exhibits. To present the Review Committee with a complete overall picture of the standards, it is generally best to prepare the generalized or summary sections first and then progress to the specific standards for individual functions or documents. This can prevent much wasted time in processing Review Committee comments on the informa-

	Summary of Initial Development Tasks	
Task	Purpose	Task Assignments
I. Develop. Schedule	1. To plan and project manpower requirements and assignments 2. To provide control points for management review. 3. To coordinate the standards effort. 4. To anticipate and tentatively schedule the implementation of sets of standards	1. Review work to be performed in detail. 2. Determine resources required and available. 3. Establish time schedule.
II. Define Policies and Procedures	1. To verify that standards will comply with management policy and other existing procedures, departmental and divisional. 2. To resolve conflicts and eliminate duplication of effort. 3. To verify that the standards effort complies with the existing management controls.	1. Review and define external policies which may affect the technical standards. 2. Identify current internal department policies and procedures. 3. Identify and review informal procedures and practices which may affect standards development. 4. Classify all unresolved or conflicting procedures in effect. 5. Resolve all above conflicts. 6. Prepare final definition of the relationship between technical standards and all other procedures

Figure 10.4 Summary of initial development tasks

	Initial Development Tasks (cont.)	
Task	Purpose	Task Assignments
III. Select Subject Sequence	1. To provide the framework for the development of a comprehensive standard package, section by section. 2. To eliminate repetition of tasks.	1. Determine priority of development. 2. Select desired approach for subject development. 3. Determine sequence of development to eliminate overlap.
IV. Cross-Reference Index	1. To assure that standards are developed in logical groups within the limitations or restrictions of the current procedures. 2. To verify that the standards will be integrated within the manual.	1. Develop a cross-reference technique, including document format. 2. Establish the relationships of the various standards and procedures now in effect. 3. List each procedure or policy that references or affects the standards, by subject matter.

Figure 10.4 (cont.)

Control Points — Project Type	Long-Term Development	Short-Term Development	Maintenance Modification	Maintenance Rescue
ANALYSIS OF TYPICAL CONTROL POINTS BY PROJECT TYPE				
1. Project Selection	X		X	
2. Project Authorization	X	X		
3. Planning	X			
4. Personnel Assignment	X			
5. Estimating	X			
6. Scheduling	X	X	X	X
7. Budgeting	X		X	
8. System Study — First Stage	X			
9. System Study — Completion	X			
10. System Analysis Completion	X			
11. System Design — Data Base	X			
12. System Design — Completion	X	X		
13. Programming — Coding Completion	X	X	X	
14. Program Testing — First Stage	X	X		
15. Program Testing — Final Stage	X	X	X	X
16. System Test Plan Completion	X			
17. System Test — Interim Stage	X			
18. System Test — Completion	X	X	X	X
19. Volume Test Plan Completion	X	X		
Project Conclusion				
20. Pre-Conversion Prep. Completion	X	X		
21. Post-Implementation Audit	X	X	X	X

Figure 10.5   Analysis of typical control points by project type

Project Type / Control Element	Project Life and Nature				Frequency of Use		
	Developmental Long Term	Developmental Short Term	Maintenance Modification	Sustaining Projects and Maintenance Rescue	Recurring Runs	On-Demand Runs	One-Time Runs
Quality	Constraint	Control Element	Constraint	Control Element			
Correctness	X	X	X	X	X	X	X
Turnover-Documentation	X	X	X		X	X	
Development Doc. (historical)	X		X		X	X	
Efficiency of System/Program	X				Dependent on run time		
Time	Flexible Element	Constraint	Flexible Element	Constraint	Start Time Only		Key Item
Resources	Control Element	Flexible Element	Control Element	Flexible Element			Total Cost Control
D. P. Staff	X		X				
Equipment	X		X				
User Staff	X						

Figure 10.6 Analysis of control elements by project type

tion which is to be presented before and after the specific subject(s) currently under review.

The comments made by the Review Committee should be evaluated by the Working Committee and a comprehensive critique of the findings and recommendations of the committee prepared. The proposed standards and the critique are then reviewed with the Review Committee and final revisions and modifications agreed.

Final Draft Preparation, Implementation Definition and Distribution

After each Review Committee meeting, the first draft is updated with the agreed revisions and amendments, and the final version of each section prepared.

Concurrently with the standards development tasks, an implementation plan should be defined. In detail, this plan should include

- identification of the methods required for the implementation of individual standards
- assignment of responsibilities for implementation tasks
- development of an implementation schedule

Part of the implementation plan should cover the prepared distribution of the standards, i.e.,

- the timing of the release of each section (or the complete manual)
- distribution criteria by level of personnel affected by the standards
- a distribution check-off list (e.g., copy numbering scheme for new material and amendment distribution)

SUMMARY

1. This chapter has presented some rules and guidelines for the preparation of documentation standards. However, it was stated a documentation standards project is usually a subject of a data processing standards program, including at least methods standards, and possibly performance standards.

2. Documentation standards development should be primarily a process of adaption rather than origination.

3. The documentation standards development program can only succeed with full management backing.

4. The output from the standards development program should be

- A Manual of Documentation Standards

- A maintenance and support program
- A training and implementation scheme

5. The development work may be divided into three distinct phases:

- Preparatory
- Development
- Part implementation

6. Each of the tasks within these three phases was broken down and discussed.

Indexed Glossary of Forms

This appendix presents a checklist of documentation in the form of an indexed glossary. Each entry shows

Document: the document name.

Reference: the major reference in the book by page number.

Prepared by)
)
Assisted by)   an example job function.
)
Approved by)

Note, however, that the project leader is assumed to approve all documentation in addition to the functions shown.

Document	Reference	Prepared by	Assisted by	Approved by
		Systems Folder		
1. User Request	25	Systems Analyst/Proponent	Proponent/Systems Analyst	Proponent
2. Systems Proposal	26		Proponent	
3. Analytical Reports	31	Project Leader/Senior Systems Analyst	Proponent	Proponent and appropriate DP management
4. Design Requirements Statement	31	Project Leader and Systems Analyst	Job/System Analysts	Proponent and DP Technical Specialists
5. Systems Summary	37	Systems Analyst	Programming Function	Programming Function
6. File Specifications	44	Systems Analyst	Programming Function	Programming Function/ Proponent
7. Transaction (Input) Specifications	53	Systems Analyst	Programming Function	Programming Function/ Proponent
8. Output Specifications	57	Systems Analyst	Proponent	Programming Function/ Proponent
9. Segment (Processing) Specification	64	Systems Analyst	Programming Function	Programming Function/ Proponent
10. Systems Test Plan	65	Systems Analyst		Project Leader/Proponent
11. Programming Specifications	89	Systems Analyst		Programming Function
		Program Folders (In Program Number Sequence)		
12. Programming Description	91	Systems Analyst		Programming Function
13. Data Specification	91	As for file, input and output specs		
14. Program Logic Specification	91	Programmer		Systems Analyst or Lead Programmer

Document	Reference	Prepared by	Assisted by	Approved by
		Program Folders (In Program Number Sequence)		
15. Listings	93	Programmer		Lead Programmer
16. Program Test Plan	95	Programmer		Systems Analyst or Lead Programmer
		Operation Folder		
17. Program Test Instructions (In Program Number Sequence)	102	Programmer		Operations Function
18. Program Operating Instructions (In Program Number Sequence)	108	Systems Analyst and Programmers		Operations Functions
19. Input Collection and Preparation Instruction	107	Systems Analyst		Point of Preparation or Collection and DP Operation
20. Input Control Instructions	109	Systems Analyst		Point of Preparation or Collection and DP Operation
21. Output Review and Distribution Instruction	109	Systems Analyst		Operations Functions
22. Output Control Instructions	109	Systems Analyst		Customer or Appropriate Directorate Responsible for Subject Matter Area

Sample Flowcharting Standards

This section presents example systems and programming flowcharting rules as they could appear in a standards manual.

SYSTEMS FLOWCHARTING

The data processing system flowchart is a symbolic representation of the processes through which data will flow in a system. The flowchart illustrates input and output requirements for each major step of the system, whether or not equipment processing is required.

To achieve a common understanding of system logic, it is desirable to adopt a standard set of symbols for use in system flowcharting.

Rules for the preparation of systems flowcharts follow.

1. All systems flowcharts must be drawn on standard XYZ company flowchart paper. A margin of one inch should be maintained on the left hand side with reasonable margins on the other sides.
2. The identification block must be completed on all flowcharts.
3. There should be one overall system flowchart for each complete system. This flowchart should, where possible, be drawn on a single sheet of A3 or A4 size paper.
4. For each sub-system, shown as a block on the overall chart, a separate chart should be drawn showing all the inputs and outputs of the sub-system including intermediate files.
5. Each block of the sub-system flowchart must be identified by a program number written on the upper right hand side and outside the symbol.

6. The logical flow of the flowchart should be from top to bottom and from left to right.

7. The direction of data flow should be shown on all connectors.

8. All system flowcharts must be drawn using the standard symbols shown in Exhibit 1. The actual size of the symbols may vary (according to the manufacturer's template employed), but the overall shape of a symbol must conform to Exhibit 1.

9. An example flowchart is shown in Exhibit 2.

PROGRAM FLOWCHARTING

A program flowchart is a symbolic representation of program logic. It serves as a communication link as well as a design tool, and must therefore have the same meaning for all data processing personnel. A uniform method of preparing flowcharts is necessary for this purpose.

There shall be at least two levels of flowchart:

1. The Macro-flowchart, which shows the major logical elements of the program.

2. Micro-flowcharts, which show the detailed logic from which the program will be written.

The relationship between the macro- and micro-flowcharts must be maintained such that each block of a macro-flowchart shall define a separate micro-flowchart, which must itself be identified by the block letter of the macro-block it represents.

Rules for the preparation of program flowcharts follow.

1. For each program, at least two levels of flowchart shall be prepared:

- Macro-flowchart
- Micro-flowchart.

2. All flowcharts shall be prepared on company XYZ flowchart paper, as shown in Exhibit 2. A margin of one inch shall be maintained on the left hand side, and reasonable margins maintained on all other sides.

3. The identification block shall be filled out whenever the form is used.

4. Only one side of the form shall be used for the preparation of flowcharts. The other side shall be left blank.

5. The flowchart symbols to be used for each operation shall, with the exception of the I/O symbols, conform to USASI standards. A list

SYSTEMS FLOWCHART SYMBOLS

1. <u>Process Symbol</u> used to represent any kind of processing function, or any operation for which no particular symbol is provided.

2. <u>Decision Symbol</u> used to represent a decision that determines which of a number of alternative paths is to be followed.

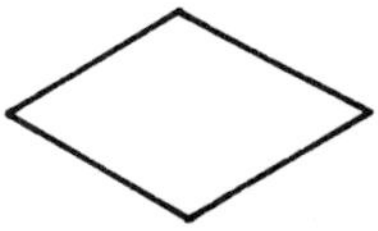

3. <u>Manual Operation Symbol</u>

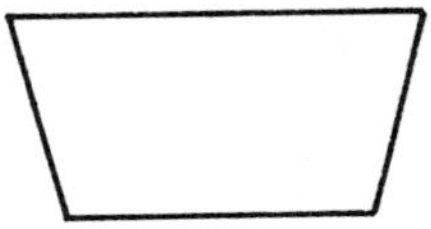

4. <u>Auxiliary Operation Symbol</u>

5. <u>Merge</u>

6. <u>Extract</u>

7. <u>Collate</u>

8. <u>Sort</u>

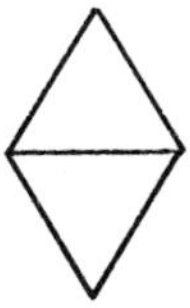

Exhibit 1   Standard symbols for system flowcharts

SYSTEMS FLOWCHART SYMBOLS

9. <u>Manual Input</u>

10. <u>Generalized Input/Output Symbol</u>

11. <u>On-Line Storage Symbol</u> represents the use of
    any kind of on-line backing, store, i.e., disc,
    drum or magnetic tape

12. <u>Off-Line Storage Symbol</u> represents the function
    of storing information off-line, regardless of the
    medium on which the data is recorded.

13. <u>Document</u>

14. <u>Punched Card</u>

15. <u>Deck of Cards</u>

16. <u>File of Cards</u>: this symbol represents a collection
    of related punched card records.

17. <u>Punched Tape</u>

18. <u>Magnetic Tape</u>

Exhibit 1 (cont.)

SYSTEMS FLOWCHART SYMBOLS

19. <u>Magnetic Drum</u>

20. <u>Magnetic Disc</u>

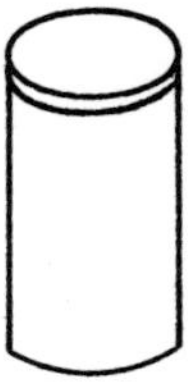

21. <u>Core Store</u>

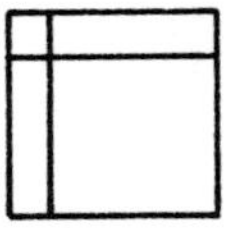

22. <u>Display</u>

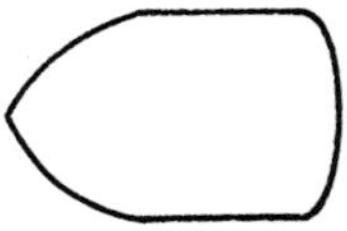

23. <u>Communication Link:</u> this symbol represents
    transfer of information by a telecommunication
    link.

24. <u>Graph Plotter</u>

25. <u>Connector</u>

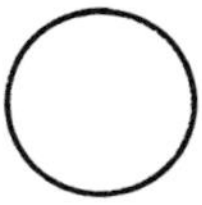

26. <u>Comment</u>

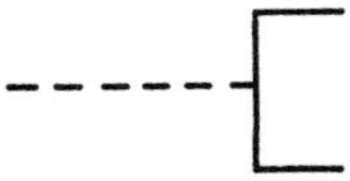

27. <u>Flow Indicators</u>

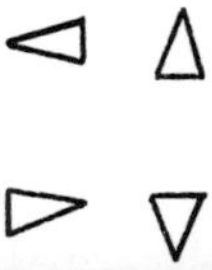

Exhibit 1 (cont.)

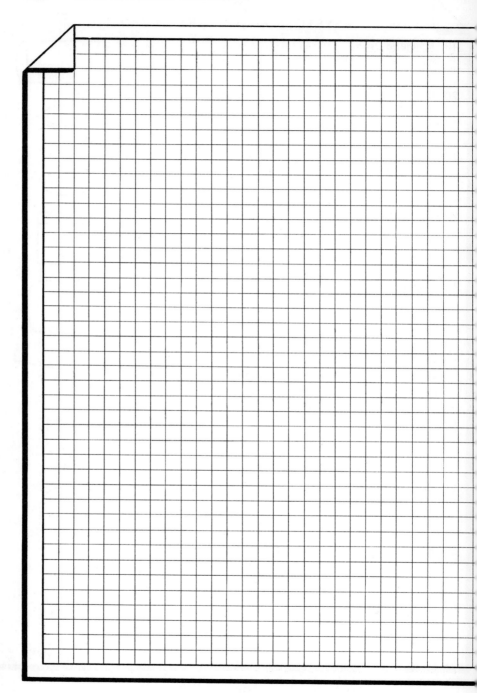

Exhibit 2   Sample flowchart

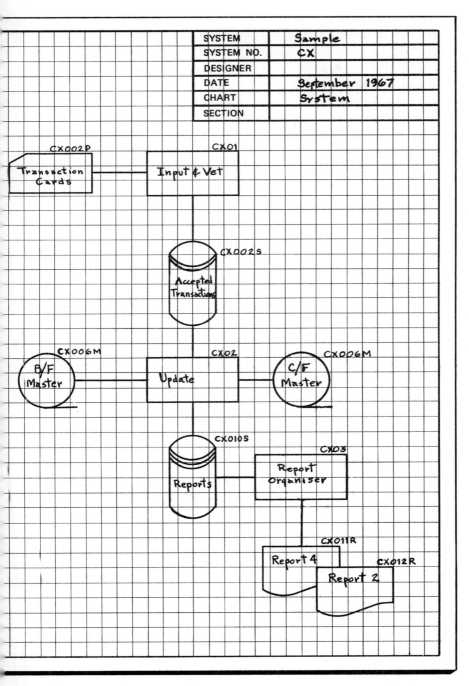

SYSTEM	Sample
SYSTEM NO.	CX
DESIGNER	
DATE	September 1967
CHART	System
SECTION	

(Two-thirds size)

of the symbols and their definitions is shown in Exhibit 3. If extra description is needed for an operation, an annotation symbol should be used.

6. The abbreviations which may be used to describe special relationships and actions on the flowcharts are shown in Exhibit 4. Any nonstandard abbreviations which are used must be defined.

7. Each block of the macro-flowchart shall be assigned an alphabetic character, starting at A and continuing sequentially to Z. The letter shall be written on the upper left hand side, and outside, the symbol. Each block of the macro-flowchart shall contain a brief description of the logic it represents.

8. For every macro-block, there will correspond a micro-flowchart. Each micro-block shall be assigned a two-digit number, starting at 01, and continuing sequentially to 99. The number shall be written outside the symbol, on the upper right hand side. Later insertions to the flowchart may be given a decimal notation within the same sequence, e.g.,

$$02.1, 02.2, \ldots, 02.8, 02.9$$

The general sequence of numbering shall as far as possible follow the logical flow of the flowchart. A brief description of the logic that each block represents shall be written inside the symbol.

9. The logical flow of the flowchart shall be from top to bottom, and left to right on the page. To avoid excessive use of connectors, this rule may be relaxed, but care should be taken that intersection of linkages is minimized. All linkages between symbols shall be shown.

10. When the logical flow of the flowchart is being maintained, arrowheads need not be shown on the linkages between symbols. When logic flows from bottom to top, or right to left of the page, arrowheads denoting the direction of flow must be shown.

11. The first symbol on each page of a micro-flowchart shall be a connector. This connector shall show the number, and the corresponding macro-block letter, of the first block on the page.

12. Each exit from a page of the micro-flowchart shall be indicated by a connector. The connector shall show the number, and the corresponding macro-block letter, of the block to which the exit is made.

Rules 11 and 12 apply also to connectors used on a sheet of flowchart where use of a linkage line is impossible (e.g., due to intersection with another linkage line).

13. Subroutines shall be shown on the micro-flowchart by use of the Predefined Process symbol. Detailed logic shall not be drawn for these

PROGRAM FLOWCHART SYMBOLS

1. General Operation Symbol: used for any operation which creates, alters, transfers or erases data, or any other operation for which no specific symbol has been defined in the Standard.

2. Subroutine (Predefined Process) Symbol: used when a section of program is considered as a single operation for the purpose of this flowchart.

3. Generalized Input/Output Symbol: used where it is desired to stress I/O operations. The symbol is used as an alternative to the specific device symbols when:
   − at the time of flowcharting the actual device to be used has not been decided,
   − the flowchart is drawn as an example, and is not related to any specific I/O function,
   − local standards specify its use.

4. Magnetic Tape I/O

5. Disc I/O

6. Drum I/O

7. Document I/O

8. Punched Card I/O

9. Punched Paper Tape I/O

Exhibit 3   Program flowcharting symbols

10. <u>Preparation Symbol</u>: used where it is desired to accentuate an operation that partially or completely determines the selection of a particular exit at given Branch Symbols.

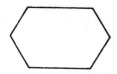

11. <u>Branch Symbol</u>: has one entry line and more than one exit. The symbol contains a description of the test on which the selection of an exit is based. The various possible results of this test are shown against the corresponding exits.

12. <u>Offpage Connector Symbol</u>: used as a linkage between two blocks of logic that are to be found on separate pages of the flowchart. The symbol is only used on the 'exit' page, on the 'entry' page an onpage symbol is used.

13. <u>Onpage Connector Symbol</u>: used as a linkage between two blocks on the same page, when it is not desirable to connect them using a linkage line. The label of the block to which the connection is being made is written inside the symbols.

14. <u>Terminal Symbol</u>: used as the beginning or end of a flowline (e.g., start or end of a program).

15. <u>Annotation Symbol</u>: used to add additional infor— mation to a symbol or block of program.

16. <u>Flowlines (Linkage Lines)</u>: used to show the flow between blocks of a flowchart. The normal flow is from top to bottom and left to right of the page. The programmer may dispense with the use of the direction arrows when the chart follows the normal flow. They must be used, however, for any portion of the diagram which does not follow the normal flow.

Exhibit 3 (cont.)

List of Standard Symbols and Abbreviations

+	Plus or positive
−	Minus or negative
±	Plus or minus, positive or negative
x	Multiplied by
÷ or /	Divided by
=	Equals
≠	Does not equal
>	Greater than
<	Less than
≥	Greater than or equal to
≤	Less than or equal to
c(x)	Contents of location X
cf or :	Compare or compared with
⟶	Used within an operational symbol to denote transfer of data
EØF	End of file
EØR	End of reel
EØJ	End of job
#	Reserved for local use
No.	Number

Exhibit 4   Standard symbols and abbreviations list

subroutines which are standard within the compiler (e.g., input/output macros) or for those subroutines which have been catalogued by Central Computer Services.

Exhibits 5 and 6 show examples of macro- and micro-flowcharts, respectively.

PROGRAM:	Tape to Printer
PROGRAM NO.	XYZ 12
PROGRAMMER	M. Brown
DATE	29.2.65
CHART:	MACRO-FLOWCHART
SECTION:	

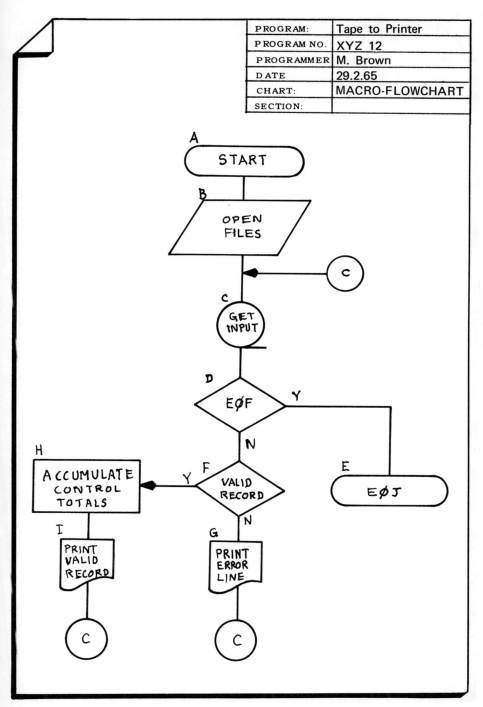

Exhibit 5   Sample Macro-flowchart

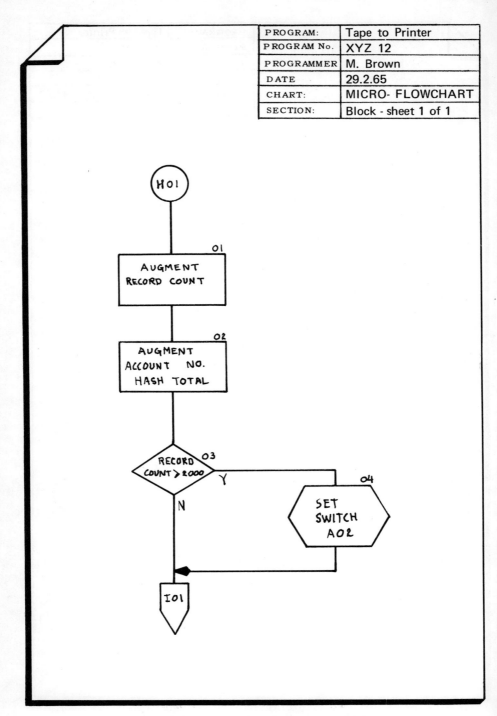

PROGRAM:	Tape to Printer
PROGRAM No.	XYZ 12
PROGRAMMER	M. Brown
DATE	29.2.65
CHART:	MICRO- FLOWCHART
SECTION:	Block - sheet 1 of 1

Exhibit 6   Sample Micro-flowchart

Standards for Decision Tables

A decision table is a tabular representation of system or program logic by defining condition/action relationships according to a set of user defined rules.

For many types of data processing problems decision tables provide a more efficient, concise and complete method of defining the system than flowcharts.

Rules for the use of decision tables follow:

1. Decision tables should be drawn on the form shown in Exhibit 1. The layout of the elements of the decision table should be:

CONDITION STUB	CONDITION ENTRY
ACTION STUB	ACTION ENTRY

The double line separating the stubs from the entries is predrawn. The designer should draw his own double line to separate condition and action areas of the form.

2. Only one table should be drawn on each sheet.

3. Tables must be named at the head of the table. A name of the form "TABLE XX" is preferred but other naming standards may be laid

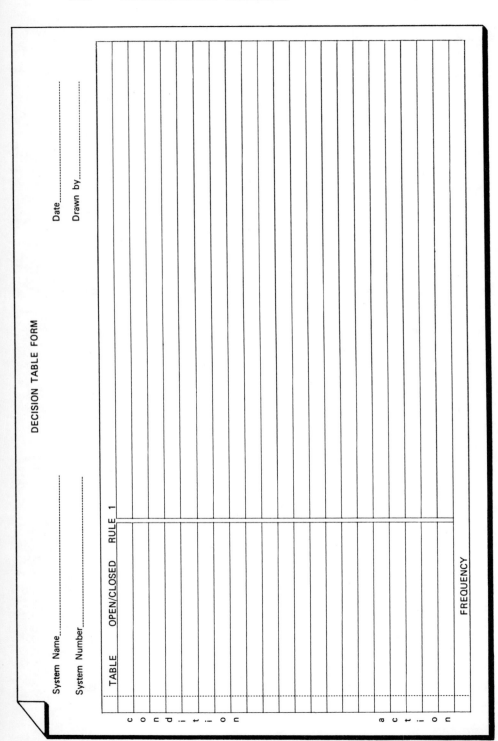

Exhibit 1 Sample decision table form

down locally. Following the name, the words OPEN or CLOSED should be written to indicate the type of table.

4. No decision table should be drawn that has:

    a. more than 4 condition variables, if neither dashes nor an ELSE rule are used, or

    b. more than 6 condition variables if dashes and/or an ELSE rule are used;

    c. more than 12 decision rules, and

    d. more than 15 action variables.

5. Blanks must not be left in the condition entries. Dashes should be used to indicate that the value of a condition does not affect a particular action.

6. On the condition entries, Y should be used to indicate the truth and N the falsity of a condition.

7. On the action entries, X should be used to indicate that an action is to be followed and I to indicate that it is to be ignored.

8. Actions must be written in the order in which they are to be executed.

9. Every effort should be made to combine rules within a table which give rise to the same action. It will often be found that the value of one condition is immaterial.

10. Tables must be drawn up in such a way that all rules are true alternatives; rules may be examined in any order but only one rule can satisfy a given set of conditions.

11. The final action entry for each rule must specify where to go next.

12. Where the information is available it can be of considerable assistance to the programmer if the expected frequency of satisfaction of each rule is indicated on the table.

13. Sample limited entry and extended entry tables are shown in Exhibits 2 and 3 respectively.

DECISION TABLE FORM

System Name: Airline Reservation Example
System Number: CX
Date: September 1967
Drawn by: R. Tomms

TABLE L3 — OPEN/CLOSED	RULE 1	2	3	4	5	6	7
c o n d i t i o n							
1 First class requested	Y	Y	Y	Y	–	–	–
2 Tourist class requested	–	–	–	–	Y	Y	Y
3 First class available	Y	N	N	N	–	Y	–
4 Tourist class available	–	Y	–	N	Y	N	N
5 Alternate class acceptable	–	–	Y	–	–	Y	N
a c t i o n							
6 Write first class ticket	X					X	
7 Write tourist class ticket		X			X		
8 Adjust 1st cl. seat invent.	X					X	
9 Adjust tourist seat invent.		X			X		
10 Suggest another flight			X	X			X
11 Go to next request	X	X			X	X	
FREQUENCY	20	8	6	10	40	9	7

Exhibit 2   Sample limited entry decision table

DECISION TABLE FORM

System Name: Airline Seat Reservation
System Number: CX

Date: September 1967
Drawn by: R. Tomms

TABLE A2 OPEN/CLOSED	RULE 1	2	3	4	5	6	7	8	9	10
c 1 Request for	First	First	First	First	First	Tourist	Tourist	Tourist	Tourist	Tourist
o 2 Space available	First	Both	Tourist	Tourist	None	Tourist	Both	First	First	None
n 3 Alternate class	-	-	OK	NG	-	-	-	OK	NG	-
d										
i										
t										
i										
o										
n										
a 4 Reduce seat inventory	First	First	Tourist	-	-	Tourist	Tourist	First	-	-
c 5 Write ticket	First	First	Tourist	-	-	Tourist	Tourist	First	-	-
t 6 Go to next	Req	Req	Req	Flight	Flight	Req	Req	Req	Flight	Flight
i										
o										
n										
FREQUENCY										

Exhibit 3   Sample extended entry decision table

INDEX